ALL
IN
GOD'S FAMILY

Brethren and the Quest for Christian Unity

ALL
IN
GOD'S FAMILY

Brethren and the Quest for Christian Unity

Fred W. Swartz

The Brethren Press, Elgin, Illinois

Library of Congress Cataloging in Publication Data

Swartz, Fred W.   1938-
  All in God's family.

  Bibliography: p.
  1. Christian union—Church of the Brethren.
I. Title.
BX7823.4.S95   262'.001   77-6375
ISBN O-87178-021-6

A LAYMAN'S LAMENT

The clergy with ease
Discuss ecumenics
The pros and cons
With faultless irenics.

But laymen, I guess
Are sunk in a bog;
We don't find our way
Through technical fog.

We don't comprehend—
(How hard have we tried?)
The ins and the outs;
Please furnish a guide!

(From the book: *A Layman's Guide to Ecumenicity,*
by Grace Douglas Orr, Lincoln, Nebraska, 1956)

CONTENTS

FOREWORD

Who cares about church unity? This question, which forms the title of the opening chapter of *All in God's Family,* reflects the mood of many in our day. The cause of ecumenism has fallen on hard days, no longer enticing either the secular or the religious press as it did in the sixties. It is reasonable to ask, as veteran ecumenist Willem Visser't Hooft does in the title of a recent book: Has the ecumenical movement a future?

Brethren will doubtless answer that question in various ways. One of the ways we have chosen to say *yes* to the question is through the Annual Conference-appointed Committee on Interchurch Relations. Successor to the older Fraternal Relations Committee, this group seeks to keep the biblical vision of unity before us—and to challenge us to act on that vision in appropriate ways.

All in God's Family is one of the most recent fruits of the work of C.I.R. It represents an attempt to find ways of working at the concern for oneness which break new ground. As the title itself indicates, the focus of the book is not on institutional mergers—but on discovering the responsibilities of a *family identity* shared with other Christians.

In an introductory chapter, a dialogue that might have taken place in any congregation tries to catch up persons "where they are." Chapters two through four locate the concern for unity squarely within the biblical witness, tracing God's dream of a family reunion as it unfolds in the

Bible. In chapters five through nine, the author takes up the fate of that dream in the church's history, including Brethren history. Chapters ten through thirteen point then to concrete ways in which we can pursue the biblical vision—in the congregation, among the Brethren, in the larger family of churches, and in the world. Suggested activities for group study can be found on pages 130-144.

The author of *All in God's Family* is Fred W. Swartz. Currently pastor of the First Church of the Brethren in Harrisburg, Pennsylvania, Fred writes as one actively involved in ecumenical relationships at the grass roots level. Together with the members of the Committee on Interchurch Relations, I believe Fred has done an outstanding job. The book is biblically rooted, deeply provocative, and highly readable.

Acknowledgement is made to the following sources for the use of quoted materials:

From *A History of the Ecumenical Movement, 1517-1948,* edited by Ruth Rouse and Stephen Charles Neill. Published in the USA by the Westminster Press, 1954, reprinted 1967. ©The Trustees of the Society for Promoting Christian Knowledge, 1953. Used by permission.

From "Visible Unity as Conciliar Fellowship," by John Deschner. *The Ecumenical Review,* January 1976. World Council of Churches.

From "Christian Unity," by Cyrille Argenti. *The Ecumenical Review,* January 1976. World Council of Churches.

From *The Student Prayerbook,* edited by J. Oliver Nelson. Haddam House, 1953. Used by permission of Association Press.

From "A Feminist's Ten Commandments," Omaha chapter of the National Organization of Women, 1975.

The Parish Ministries Commission of the Church of the Brethren General Board is happy to co-sponsor the publication of *All in God's Family.* We look forward to its wide usage by both individuals and congregational study groups.

Rick Gardner, Editor

Chapter 1

Who Cares About Church Unity?

Mr. Brown is the resource leader for the General Adult Elective Church School Class at Faith Avenue Church of the Brethren, Serenity, New York. His pupils are strictly volunteer: Some attend to get away from the traditional, others come because of the relational subjects, and a few just "sit in" out of admiration for Mr. Brown. The class is largely middle-aged persons, complemented by a sampling of younger and older adults. Mr. Brown tries to be democratic in the selection of study content and tests anyone's suggestions with the reactions of the class members.

Mr. Brown: "Mary has suggested that we should turn our attention in this class toward a study of the relationship of our denomination to the other churches. The sixty-four-dollar word for this is "ecumenism," studying similarities and differences of the various communions in Christendom and where we stand on Christian unity. How do you feel about giving this priority for our time and study?"

Mary: "I suggested it because I'm always hearing rumors that the Brethren are going to merge with some other church, and I'm not sure I like that idea. I mean, most of the other denominations are so large, and if we would merge I'm afraid we'd be the little fish. I've been Brethren all my life.

"Of course my husband thinks all churches are the same and it really doesn't matter which one you belong to. He says we'll all wind up at the same place someday and there won't be denominations *there!* I guess he has a point!"

Ruby: Well, I'm sure of one thing—our church certainly isn't like the *Catholics!* You know our daughter, Jean, is going to marry a Catholic boy. I guess we'll lose her from our faith. Sam and I just hate to think of our grandchildren being brought up in a *different religion* than ours. She certainly ought to know Brethren doctrine, though; we never missed a Sunday bringing her to Sunday school when she was a girl."

Harry: "It's a lot freer now among the churches, though. I remember when we couldn't have anyone else from another denomination attend our love feast. We had some company in our home one love feast weekend several years, ago, and we just stayed home that Sunday, knowing we couldn't invite them. I'm sure glad we don't have that rule anymore. It's a crying shame if all Christians can't eat together at the Lord's table!"

Jacob: "Yeah ... of course my wife's folks are Lutheran and I've had communion at their church a couple of times. It just isn't the same without the full love feast. But my father-in-law thinks we're crazy for washing feet. It's just something we can't see eye to eye on."

George: "That's true. I don't believe there'll ever be one church. I know the fellows at work can't understand what pacifism is. They say God doesn't intend for us to let somebody run all over us, and they're glad their churches

12

don't preach that. Anyway, they don't believe that everything Jesus said is relevant for our modern age. They say you have to adapt it to the reality of today. I think they'd have a hard time in the Church of the Brethren, and maybe we wouldn't want them anyway!"

Mabel: "But isn't the church supposed to be for everybody? I certainly hope we have a church here where everybody can feel at home."

Joe: "I disagree with you, Mabel. People have different tastes and needs. It's impossible to have one church that suits everybody. I think we're just spinning wheels to talk about 'ecoomism,' or however you pronounce it. Most people want to stay where they are, or in the church they grew up in. I think Jesus intended to have denominations when he picked twelve disciples. Each one of them was going to give his own interpretation to Jesus' words, wasn't he?

"But even practically speaking, unity is impossible. Denominations have existed far too long to ever get together. We'd do well if we could just unify our own church a little. If you ever get to an Annual Conference you'll see what I mean: the difference just in the Church of the Brethren, even down to the clothes! Why I saw delegates in everything from shorts to the plain garb! And then there always seem to be several different groups that want their viewpoints to be heard on every issue. When you see so much division *within* a denomination, you can see why denominations could never make peace!"

John: "That reminds me of the cliques Paul identifies in the Corinthian Church. I guess there's been division in the Church from the beginning. If they couldn't achieve unity then, can we expect to now, after 2000 years of differences?"

Sarah: "Maybe it depends on what you mean by 'unity.' I agree with Joe—I don't think God expects everybody to think alike, or even worship alike. He certainly took

13

" . . . but isn't the church supposed to be for everybody?"

pains to insure that no two persons are carbon copies *physically*. . . . But doesn't the Bible stress a certain kind of oneness in Christ, a common base from which we all work, albeit in diverse ways, toward the same goal of bringing God's kingdom on earth?"

Frank: "Maybe so, but that raises a point I'd like settled. How do you know if a church or a so-called 'Christian' group is working from the true foundation? Some of these outfits I hear over the radio, or see their ads in the newspaper, I have my doubts about. I'm suspicious of any groups that don't belong to a mainline denomination."

Sarah: "Aren't the mainline churches *trying* to work more together, though? It seems like I've heard a lot about the councils of churches lately. And we do cooperate in things like clothing for relief and the SOS offering at Thanksgiving."

Tom: "Hmph! the Council of Churches is nothing more than a lot of worthless talk! Get two or three of the large denominations in there and they run the whole show. I think churches would get along better if they're just left to work together in each community, instead of having some bunch of desk-leaners in New York try to tell us what to do. I'm not so sure but what they aren't right about those outfits being Communist!"

Rachel: "But Tom, it just doesn't happen in the local community. Why you remember our committee meeting with the Church of Christ and the Methodists to try to plan a cooperative Bible School. We couldn't even agree on what version of the Bible to use in the classes. And when each of the pastors wanted to have the school at *his* church, that killed our attempt at cooperation! I don't know, but I think if we ever make any progress at church unity it will have to be at the top, where the executives don't have to bother with congregations that are set in their ways!"

John: "Don't you think that for a lot of people the church name with which they grew up is an integral part of their faith? I think if the Church of the Brethren were to merge with another denomination and we'd have another name, a lot of people would be pretty shook up!"

Mabel: "But that shouldn't be! Our loyalty ought to be to Christ and not to a tradition or a particular set of doctrines. That's our trouble now! Persons interpret religion according to what suits them rather than the Bible. How can there be more than one way to represent and worship Christ?"

Mr. Brown: "It seems evident enough that Mary has suggested a subject that reveals a variety of experiences and opinions among our class. You have raised a number of questions about biblical material. Perhaps that's the place we ought to start, and see if we can discover a biblical pattern for the church.

Chapter 2

God's Dream
of a Family Reunion

Remember family reunions? They used to be an annual summertime delight for this writer in his boyhood! It was the only time (with the exception of funerals) that the whole clan was together, both physically and emotionally. The differences of opinion that floated about through rumors during the year, the estate squabbles, jealousies, offenses, past embarrassments to the family honor—all of this was put on the back burner, at least for the major part of the afternoon! There was a sharing of food, a lot of un-usual courtesies, exchanges of snapshots, and even a soft-ball game without regard to generation or sex differences!

But most importantly of all, those family reunions promoted a sense of *belonging*. You had a *place* in this group that no one else could fill: You were the "son of so-and-so? Oh yes, then your grandfather was . . . . My, my, how you've grown up." For certain, those reunions provid-ed a reference for identity for the children (and probably some of the adults, too), giving visible credence to the verbal maze of cousins and uncles and great-aunts. And all around you could hear the ring of satisfying triumph as the family tree was successfully re-erected (for the ten-thousandth time), uniting "Cousin Jane" and "Cousin Christine" under the same great-grandfather. *Reunion* was indeed the right appellation for those events!

Is it possible to talk about a reunion of the entire human family, to bring together every man, woman, and child from every corner and land upon the earth, in a joyous celebration of kinship and peace and sharing? Physically, such a feat would be impractical, if we continue to think of the model by which our family namesakes annually gather. Not even the Astrodome, with its preposterous title, could accomodate us!

Recently an adult church school teacher got bogged down in his interpretation of the last judgment in Matthew 25 when he came to verse 32: "Before him will be gathered *all the nations* . . . " Our teacher had suddenly registered some sort of perspective on the size gathering "all the nations" would be. He was about ready to scrap the whole passage on the basis that it would be impossible to find a place where the whole population of earth could be assembled. Obviously our teacher needs some help in understanding symbolic language. But at least he was beginning to get a feel for the magnitude of the human family!

The reunion we are envisioning is not that of a "convention for everybody." Rather, it is a reunion in terms of identity, common purpose, and relationship. Is it possible to reunite the earth's people in such a way that we can move in and out freely and peaceably with one another? Can we share equally in the resources available for the whole family's needs, so that each will be honored with a rightful and unique place?

To talk about a *reunion* of the human family presupposes two things: (1) That there is one universal human

18

"family." (2) That the human family has in fact experienced fragmentation.

The first of the two suppositions is often the most difficult to accept, for stereotyped prejudice stands in the way. Prejudice undermines the logic of kinship in our consideration of others. National or cultural peculiarities become stereotypes for each person, until we are convinced that "they" are different, not like us. Therefore, we choose to live, associate with, "take a wife from" our own kind, and we ostracize those who do not conform to this norm.

Yet all the evidence points toward a deep kinship among human beings. We may begin by citing physical likenesses and common physiological and emotional needs such as shelter, food, love, and security. Culturally we are increasingly interdependent on one another as the world's population swells and the earth's resources dwindle. The technical advances of television and satellite communication have literally brought the world into the living room.

But there is also a religious base for recognizing a world family. No cultural or national group of humans has ever been without a faith of some sort. From primitive times on there has been a consistent search for, and identification with, a supreme being—a being outside of, and more powerful, than humans. This being has consistently been described in such ways as the Creator, the Sustainer of life, and the Judge and Ruler of all creation.

The assumption of a universal human family is shared by the biblical writers. According to the Bible, God conceived humankind as a unity from the very beginning. The first "Man" (Adam) was representative of all human beings to follow in creation. The second "Man" (Christ) is also referred to by Paul as being the symbol (as well as the agent) of the will of God for *all* people. (See also Romans 5:12-20). Furthermore, Paul affirms that God is no respecter of persons (Gal. 3:28). His aspirations, expec-

" . . . the assumption of a universal human family is shared by the biblical writers."

tations, and love are meted out equally to each of his children. There are no degrees of difference in status or privilege. While individually each person is unique, collectively there are no favorites. All are part of the family he creates.

The second presupposition of talk about reunion mentioned above is all too evident. In spite of its potential unity and kinship, the human family has experienced separation and alienation from its inception. Not even the first genetic family could peacefully co-exist, as Cain killed his brother Abel in a fit of jealousy (Gen. 4:1-16). The biblical story reflects primitive relationships as constantly going from bad to worse. Thus we read in Genesis 6:11: "Now the earth was corrupt in God's sight, and the earth was filled with violence."

Even after the flood co-existence was a problem, a problem compounded by conspirative pride, manifest in the attempt at building a tower "with its top in the heavens." The result of this ill-fated venture was the separation of offended families from one another until they were disbursed to isolated parts of the world (Gen. 11). Opting to control their own lives, humans find their ship swerves wildly. Assuming selfish autonomy, they forget their common origin.

Fortunately, the biblical story does not end here. The very title of this chapter presupposes that God desires to bring together those who are cut off. God has a dream or vision of family reunion. Eager to restore humanity to the sense of fraternal kinship he intended from the beginning, God calls Abraham to a special mission:

> Now the Lord said to Abram, "Go from your country and your kindred and your father's house to the land that I will show you. And I will make of you a great nation, and I will bless you, and make your name great, so that you will be a blessing. I will bless those who bless you, and him who curses you I will curse; and by you all the families of the earth shall bless themselves."
>
> (Genesis 12:1-3)

21

As the covenant between God and Abraham is repeated in subsequent scriptures, it consistently includes a blessing for "all the nations." Through this particular covenant with a genetic family, God was attempting to reunite the relational family of those with a common origin in his image. It was the purpose of the first patriarch, as well as that of the subsequent generations of Israel, to sound the call and provide the nucleus around which all the tribes on earth would gather in recognition of their common identity and spiritual nature.

One of Abraham's first crises in his mission is symbolic of this role, as he moves to avoid brokenness with Lot:

> Then Abram said to Lot, "Let there be no strife between you and me, and between your herdsmen and my herdsmen; for we are kinsmen. Is not the whole land before you? Separate yourself from me. If you take the left hand, then I will go to the right; or if you take the right hand, then I will go to the left."
>
> (Genesis 13:8-9)

In spite of the strong national exclusiveness maintained by the Hebrews during the monarchial era, the major prophets championed God's hope for a family reunion. The eighth century (B.C.) prophet Micah anticipated a day when the peoples of the earth would be united in one world of justice, law, and peace (4:1-7). All alike looking to the word of the Lord going forth from Jerusalem, nations would no longer take up the sword against each other. There would be respect for each other's rights and freedom from fear. Those driven away and cast off in earlier days would be reunited with people.

This hope for a family reunion is most pronounced in Second Isaiah, for example Isaiah 49:5-6:

> And now the Lord says,
>   who formed me from the womb to be his servant,
> to bring Jacob back to him,
>   and that Israel might be gathered to him,
> For I am honored in the eyes of the Lord,
>   and my God has become my strength—
> he says:

"It is too light a thing that you should be my servant
    to raise up the tribes of Jacob
    and to restore the preserved of Israel:
I will give you as a light to the nations,
    that my salvation may reach to the end of the earth."

The prophet speaks to the despair of an exiled people, declaring that God will again deliver the nation and restore freedom to their descendants. But there is a very important aspect to that future blessing—the nation will serve as witness to *all the world* to the authority and salvation of God (49:6). Furthermore, there shall be an ingathering of new members into the community of Israel, the implication being that they shall come from outside the tribal relation:

They shall spring up like grass amid waters,
    like willows by flowing streams.
This one will say, 'I am the Lord's,
    another will call himself by the name of Jacob,
and another will write on his hand, 'The Lord's'
    and surname himself by the name of Israel.

                        (Isaiah 44:4-5)

Henry Sloan Coffin comments about these verses: "In this instance the poet sees these heathen from the nations seeking incorporation in the spiritual Israel" (*Interpreter's Bible,* Vol. 5, p. 503). The emphasis is upon the creation of a spiritual community in which all people together recognize and celebrate the name of God.

But the prophets were lonely men, whose message went largely unheard or unheeded. It was the failure of God's covenant people to grasp their universal mission that necessitated the incarnation (cf. Heb. 1:1). By the time of Christ the Jews were a proud people, extremely protective of their heredity. Their religion, with its multitude of rules and prescribed standards, was designed to be exclusive. It was harder for Gentiles to break into the Jewish camp in the first century than it was for the English and the Italians to find acceptance among the German Baptist Brethren in the nineteenth century!

Into this world of alien relationships came the Son of God with the word of reconciliation. In truth, he *was* the reconciler, the One through whom the reunion of humans with God and with one another would be effected:

> He is the image of the invisible God, the first-born of all creation; for in him all things were created, in heaven and on earth, visible and invisible, whether thrones or dominions or principalities or authorities—all things were created through him and for him. He is before all things, and in him all things hold together. He is the head of the body, the church; he is the beginning, the first-born from the dead, that in everything he might be preeminent. For in him all the fullness of God was pleased to dwell, and through him to reconcile to himself all things, whether on earth or in heaven, making peace by the blood of his cross.
>
> (Colossians 1:15-20)

This new community in Christ was manifested right within the first great gathering of the church on the day of Pentecost. There were Jews present from all parts of the ancient world, and *proselytes,* Gentiles from Crete and Arabia. Apparently for the first time in their experience, either religious or secular, they discovered a common bond transcending and overshadowing their cultural and geographical differences. Their question to one another, "What does this mean?" (Acts 2:12) was definitely more an exclamation of wonder than an appeal for explanation.

The Pentecost event must have resembled the warm feeling of kinship and love that accompanies the prayer group where an intimate, supportive fellowship is developed in Christian love and trust. People from "every nation under heaven" were together, their differences overcome, for the simple reason that their focus was upon One whose life and love surpassed and defeated the forces which divided them. God had taken the biggest gamble in history to bring about the fulfillment of his dream. He had demonstrated through sacrifice of his Son his love for the whole world.

For God so loved the world that he gave his only Son, that

24

whoever believes in him should not perish but have eternal life. For God sent the Son into the world, not to condemn the world, but that the world might be saved through him.

(John 3:16-17)

Chapter 3

The Barriers Begin to Fall

The central message of the New Testament is that Christ, through his life on earth, his death, and his resurrection has brought reconciliation between man and God and between men. Those who accept him as their lord live in a new dimension and a new community in which love and unity are regnant. This unity is not only spiritual; it pervades life in all its relationships, it continually refashions the life of the church and it seeks even to permeate and remake human society.

(Listen Pope, *The Kingdom Without Caste,* p. 156)

We ended chapter 2 with a reference to John 3:16-17: "For God so loved the world that he gave his only Son . . . that the world might be saved through him." These two verses are like a mini-editorial in the midst of the Fourth Evangelist's narrative, offering commentary on the purpose of the event of Christ, The foci are two: the Son, and the world to and for whom the Son was sent. The breadth of Jesus' mission is implied. He was not a Messiah for one nation alone; he was not sent only to good people, nor a redeemer of only those who responded favorably to him.

26

He came to save the whole world and to draw *all* people into the heavenly fold.

Jesus' entire ministry reflected his mission as God's emissary to all people, associating with despised groups and individuals without discrimination. He taught about the one Father of all ("Our Father, who art in heaven . . . "). He illustrated neighborliness for his predominately Jewish audience by telling a story of an exemplary act by a Samaritan, one of their heretical cousins to the north. Furthermore, he instructed his disciples to preach the gospel "to all nations," and he predicted that when he was lifted up in final glory he would draw *all* persons to himself (John 12:35-36).

That Jesus was sent by God to fulfil the mission God had intended for the descendants of Abraham is clear in one of the earliest incidents in Jesus' itinerant ministry (Matt. 8:5-13). As he entered the city of Capernaum he was approached by a Roman centurion, one of seven such military career men mentioned in Matthew and Acts as relating in some sympathetic way to the Christian movement. The centurion had a special and desperate request of Jesus: "My slave is dying. Won't you help him?"

That request in itself was remarkable, for slaves were classed in the same category as animals. The common practice when an owner had a sickly slave was to dismiss him or try to sell him. The master had no obligation whatsoever to see that the slave received medical attention. But the Capernaum centurion apparently felt compassion and personal concern for his slave, perhaps already some manifestation of the reconciling mood to be set by Jesus.

A second striking feature of this story is the fact that the centurion would approach a Jewish teacher. Centurions were Gentiles, and thus considered by the Jews to be of a lower estate. Jews were not to cross the threshold of the home of a non-Jew, because Gentile dwellings were considered unclean (i.e. not *ceremonially* fit for God's service and presence). The centurion was well acquainted with this injunctive and alludes to it, saying to Jesus, "I am not fit for you to enter my house, but just give the command from here and my servant will be healed" (Matt. 8:8).

It is obvious that Jesus is greatly impressed with the centurion's faith. According to Matthew, Jesus uses the occasion to announce the breadth of the family of God. He does so by rather daringly describing the nature of the Messianic banquet. The Jews eagerly anticipated a great spiritual feast, hosted by the Messiah, at which the whole nation, both past and present, would sit down to toast victory over all their foes. That the non-Jewish or anti-Jewish world might participate in the Messianic banquet was an uncommon view. So Jesus shocks his hearers by proclaiming that "many will come from the east and west" while some of the "sons of the kingdom" (i.e. Jews) will be rejected as guests. Clearly, the kingdom of God was not the possession of any one group or nation.

Jesus also moved to destroy the sex barrier which prescribed separate statuses for men and women in the first century. In both the Judaistic and the Greek cultures woman was considered to be man's inferior. While there are evidences that individual women ofttimes rose above that status, they were also vulnerable victims of its frequent enforcement. For instance, if a man tired of his wife and desired another, he could divorce the first almost without a reason.

In the practice of *religion* women were at an even greater disadvantage, ranking with slaves in their privileges and duties. Theology was considered the sport and preoccupation of men (at least in the public square) and women were to "keep quiet in church."

Jesus had no hesitancy about engaging women in conversation about faith. (See Luke 10:38-42 and John 4:1-26.) And his acceptance toward all people and all ages enabled him to be a teacher to whom women were unafraid to reach out and touch (see Mark 5:24-34). Arthur John Gossip writes:

> It was Christ who gave woman her chance, who saw her possibilities, who discovered her value. . . . It was Christ who discovered and emphasized the worth of a woman. It was Christ who lifted her into equality with man: not, indeed, into sameness of duty, for nature itself precludes that. Yet, as Paul has it, in Christ there is neither male nor female in the sense that both alike are dear to God, and both alike are called to the service of the kingdom, and both alike can and should reach the same lofty spiritual goals.
>
> (*Interpreter's Bible,* Vol. 8, p. 530)

If Jesus were choosing the Twelve today, there would in all likelihood be some women among the group.

The story of Jesus' encounter with the woman of Samaria witnesses to his acceptance of people from all nations and strata. It also shows Jesus' example was beginning to change the disciples' point of view. The incident at historic Jacob's well (John 4:1-16) happened as Jesus and his traveling company were making a long desert trek from Judea to Galilee, a journey that included a stretch of Samaria. What makes this route so critical is the fact of a centuries-old feud between the Jews and the Samaritans.

The staunch and legalistic Jews considered their Samaritan cousins the wayward sheep of the "family," for they had intermarried with the Assyrians following the Assyrian invasion of Samaria in 720 B.C.. By introducing "foreign blood" into the tribe the Samaritans had lost their hereditary purity. Their rejection by the southern Jews was cemented in 450 B.C., when the Samaritans were not allowed to help the returning exiles from Babylon rebuild the Jerusalem temple. They were scolded for betraying their Jewish heritage and told that their help was not needed.

The affection gap widened when the Samaritans established their own temple on Mount Gerizim and touted

" . . . Jesus' encounter with the woman of Samaria witnesses to his acceptance of people from all nations and strata."

it as Jerusalem's rival. The resulting jealousy led to an embittered war in 129 B.C. when John Hyrcanus, the Jewish general and leader, directed an attack upon Samaria and destroyed the northern temple. By the time of Jesus the Jews and the Samaritans held absolute contempt for one another.

It is noteworthy that Jesus would even choose to journey through Samaria. The danger to a Jewish traveler through that territory was comparable to the potential calamities the typical white middle-class churchman imagines will befall him if he drives alone through the ghetto at night. But Jesus knows no enemies. (He even looked upon those who crucified him with compassion and interceded for their pardon, Luke 23:34.) He who would not avoid Jerusalem had no fear of Samaria. He did not share the animosity of his countrymen against the north.

The Samaritan woman expresses astonishment that Jesus (a Jew) would even *look* her way, much less speak to her. But to Jesus she was another person in need of freedom from sin's bondage. That was of far greater urgency than external cultural and ideological differences. William Barclay comments on this passage in his *Daily Study Bible:* "Here was Jesus breaking through the nationality and orthodox Jewish custom. Here is the beginning of the universality of the gospel; here is God so loving the world, not in theory, but in action" (*The Gospel of John,* Vol. 1, p. 143).

The attitude of the disciples is a sub-plot within the story. Not only were they accompanying Jesus through Samaria. While he stopped to rest at the well they unhesitantly went on ahead to purchase some food in the nearest town. It would indicate that they were beginning to catch the spirit of the universal Christ. Being Jews, they would never before have considered entering a Samaritan town even as tourists, not to mention as consumers! And when they return to where they had left the Master, they apparently are not shocked to see a Jew and a Samaritan discussing religion. They only marvel that Jesus is sharing a conversation of faith matters with a woman. The barriers were melting in the heat of Jesus' love for the inner person.

Jesus extended that same nondiscriminatory love to those who were branded as outcasts and untouchables in his day. He took time to visit with Zacchaeus to invite this isolated man into the fellowship of the redeemed (Luke 19:1-10). "For the Son of man came to seek and to save the lost," Luke quotes him as saying (19:10). Perhaps this is the origin of the modern idiom, "The church is a hospital for sinners, not a haven for saints."

Jesus walked right up to lepers and touched them, while others crossed the street to avoid them. He healed on the Sabbath, putting people before traditions. He marveled at examples of deeper faith in some of the outcasts and Gentiles than he witnessed in the so-called religious people (cf. Luke 7:1-9, 36-50).

Paul testified that in Christ, "there is neither Jew nor Greek, slave nor free, male or female, for all are one in Christ Jesus" (Gal. 3:28). Jesus came to overcome the differences and shatter the barriers that separate the family of God and to invite all to share together at the Messianic banquet of salvation.

Chapter 4

The New Family Becomes Visible

A fascinating childhood discovery occurs when one casts a stone into a pool of tranquil water for the first time. The penetration of the object into the placid surface results in a multiplying series of concentric circles, until the effect of the stone reaches from "shore to shore." Such an analogy might well be used to view the effect of the "family-style" march of early Christianity.

Luke records in Acts 1:8 his version of Jesus' Great Commission: "You shall be my witnesses—in Jerusalem and in all Judea and in Samaria and to the farthest bounds of the earth." There is no mistaking how far, nor how inclusive the disciples' witness was to be. Like the round ripples surrounding the stone's dunking, the circles of Christian witness were to start in Jerusalem, then expand outward. Beginning in Judea, they would proceed on to Samaria, a semi-Jewish area, and finally encircle even the heathen world. The bounds of the family were universal.

As the story of Acts unfolds before the reader's eyes, the concentric circles take real form. Acts 2:1 strikes the key note: "They were all together in one place." That oneness, that community, is emphatically visible in the organizing stages of the Christian movement. The earliest believers professed to be one people.

The strong sense of unity was expressed in several ways: First, in mutual sharing and respect. "And all who believed were together and had all things in common; and they sold their possessions and goods and distributed them to all, as any had need" (Acts 2:44-45). Even outsiders recognized the Christians' love for one another as a distinctive mark of their fellowship. Oft quoted is a remark attributed to Tertullian in the second century: "See how these Christians love one another."

There was a unity of faith. The earliest confession was a simple one: "Jesus is Lord," yet it said it all: acceptance of Jesus as the Messiah, both a key to the heritage of the scriptures and a "bright hope for tomorrow." The first apostles were exuberantly possessed with the urgent and good news of the gospel, " . . . for we cannot but speak of what we have heard and seen" (Acts 4:20). Its proclamation and celebration took priority even over the preservation of life and limb.

There was a unity of worship. From the beginning the Christians observed two distinctly new ordinances: breaking of bread and baptism. Paul in Ephesians (4:5) cites the *one baptism* as one of the factors in the unity of the church, and Luke speaks of a united devotion to "the apostles' teaching and fellowship, to the breaking of bread and the prayers" (Acts 2:42). The breaking of bread must surely be the primitive beginnings of the Eucharist, the sacrament that is still a universal practice throughout Christendom. Baptism not only sealed the surrender of a believer but also signaled the transition from an old order to a new world order in which God is gathering all things together into unity with Jesus Christ.

There was a unity that manifested itself in a new trusting relationship. One is impressed in reading Acts how freely the Christians come and go among one another. In the first century the zeal of an authentic believer was of such convincing magnitude that he was automatically recognized as a member of the Christian community no matter where he travelled. Even when they differed in principle the Christians still regarded each other as brothers and sisters.

These beautiful factors of a community—a commonness of life, faith, worship, love and trust—were laying the foundation for the reconciling mission of the Christian movement. The stone was dropped in Jerusalem, the mother church, where the first group of disciples and followers experienced the circle of love. What a powerful impact upon the stagnant waters of the Greco-Roman world the Christian penetration would have!

Already in Acts 6 we see the expanding influence of "family-style" Christianity. The temple membership in the first century consisted of two classes of Jews—those who resided in Jerusalem and Palestine and spoke Aramaic, and those who were from foreign countries and had adopted Greek ways and speech. The Palestinian Jews regarded themselves as the purely orthodox and held contempt for the wayward Greek-speaking Jews. This contempt spilled over into the distribution of alms to the widows, apparently the widows of the foreign Jews who had come to Jerusalem to live. These widows were being neglected in the distribution.

As the Christians adopted the alms practice of their own fellowship, they took precautions to make sure *all shared fairly* in the distribution, regardless of their origin or status. Furthermore, seven men were appointed to act as deacons, not one of whom had a Jewish name. One, Nicolaus, is even singled out as a Gentile from Antioch who had embraced the Jewish faith. Already barriers to human separation are falling. Not only are both Aramaic and Hellenist Jews being treated alike in the new fellowship. The latter, who barely commanded even a glance of respect in the temple, were also trusted with responsible positions.

One of the seven deacons, Stephen, is gifted with unusual foresight. He is among the first to envision Christianity embracing the whole world. He accuses the Jews of limiting God to one place (Jerusalem) when in truth God is Lord of the whole universe. No group has a corner on his grace and love.

The seeds for an inclusive human family had been definitely sown. How dramatic that one of these seeds, thanks to the prayer and attitude of Stephen, fell upon the barren, rocky soil of Saul's heart, later to produce the apostle laureate to the Gentiles!

But Paul's time is not yet. There are some other circles to come in between. Acts 8 is a supremely important chapter in the unfolding outreach of the church. Saul's purge of the Christian followers sends the faithful to safer areas (Acts 8:1). But it did not, it could not, quell their enthusiasm and witness! One of Stephen's fellow deacons, Philip, preaches Christ to the Samaritans, the hillbilly cousins of the Palestinian Jews. To Philip the centuries-old feud between Jews and Samaritans was superseded by the urgent mission of Christ. That the church was beginning to move beyond the previously-held stigma of race and class is further illustrated by the response of the mother church in Jerusalem to the news of the Samaritan mission. It sent *Peter and John,* the two foremost apostles, the two top officials in the cabinet, to undergird the new fellowship.

The Hellenistic deacon, Philip, is not yet through with his pioneering. Upon an inspired impulse he takes a journey south of Jerusalem in the direction of Egypt.

There he meets an Ethiopian eunuch, a man in charge of a North African queen's treasury and who is also a Jewish proselyte. Philip has opportunity to interpret Isaiah 53 for him and to lead him to an acceptance of Jesus. The international family of God continues to grow and the circles expand a little larger.

Then comes Luke's most important story in the drama of the universal family in Christ. Acts 10:1-16 tells of Peter's encounter with Cornelius, the centurion of Caesarea, two very unlikely persons to have such close dialogue and fellowship. Cornelius was a Gentile, an uncircumcised Jewish proselyte; and Peter was a full-fledged, duly accredited Jew. The strict Jew believed that God had no use for Gentiles, and consequently Jews were to have no contact with a Gentile. Jews were neither to accept hospitality from or give hospitality to a Gentile. How unorthodox, then, Peter's action. He receives the couriers sent by Cornelius to beseech him to come, and upon arriving in Caesarea Peter does not hesitate to cross the centurion's doorstep.

Here we see Christianity, in its foremost adherent, breaking down the barriers that separate God's human family. Peter's association with Jews had given him pause to evaluate the formidable barriers of sectarian Judaism. Already he had discovered some of these restrictions stifling and artificial. It is not merely coincidental that the vision in which he was commanded to eat the meat of unclean animals (Acts 10:9-16) came to him while he was a guest in the home of a tanner. The trade of a tanner, who handled dead bodies, was considered unclean, and the most orthodox of Jews would have never accepted hospitality in a tanner's home.

So Peter was ready to break out of his narrowness, and Cornelius was searching for meaning. Luke dramatically suggests that the divine hand of God brought the two together in a convincing demonstration of equality and

37

unity. That Luke attaches great importance to this incident is evidenced in his repeating every detail in the story when Peter explains his action back in Jerusalem. The author correctly sees this event as the turning point between Christianity as an ethnic sect and Christianity becoming a world-wide faith.

Now Luke can reveal how the dispersed witnesses are already preaching to the Gentiles in Asia Minor and Cyprus (Acts 11:19-21). It has taken several concentric circles, but the splash has been completed:

> The fellowship at Jerusalem
> Philip preaching to the Samaritans
> Peter baptizing Cornelius
> The gospel preached to the Gentiles

Christianity is now launched on its world-wide mission, and the new family is becoming visible.

The Antioch congregation is representative of the reclaimed community. Antioch was the third largest city of the world at that time and typically cosmopolitan. The list of church leaders illustrates this very point (Acts 13:1-3): Barnabas, a Jew from Cyprus; Lucius, from Cyrene in North Africa; Simeon, a Jew with a Roman name as well, Niger; and Manaen, an aristocrat. Paul also spent much time with the Antioch group and he was a Jew from Tarsus in Cilicia and a trained rabbi. The church at Antioch proved that persons from many backgrounds and cultures can find unity and togetherness in the spirit of Christ.

Furthermore, it is worth noting that the spirit was such in Antioch that, upon hearing a prediction of a forthcoming famine in Judea, the fellowship lifted a relief offering, to be sent to the Jerusalem Church (Acts 11:27-30). The incident foreshadows the collection Paul will later take up in the Gentile churches and points to the solidarity early Christian congregations felt with fellow communities of believers.

The inclusive spirit of the Christian movement is

demonstrated in various ways in the cities Paul visits in his missionary journeys. At Philippi (Acts 16:6-26) Paul succeeds in converting a wide cross-section of the population, from the wealthy merchant, Lydia, to a slave girl on the bottom rung of society's ladder. In Athens (Acts 17:16-21) Paul begins preaching without regard for whether these strange people would "fit into" the fellowship of the rest of the church. They are people who haven't heard the story; they need adoption into the family. At Corinth (Acts 17:32-34) Paul faces perhaps his most difficult task, preaching to a city immersed in wickedness and worldliness. How hard he worked to win the Corinthians and keep them in the household of God! At Ephesus, he had to buck pagan superstition and preach the goodness of Jesus in a city that was an asylum for criminals. But to them he later writes, "You are fellow citizens with the saints and members of the household of God" (Eph. 2:19).

The more one studies the story and activity of the apostle Paul, the more one marvels at the man's industry and ingenuity. Not only was he a master in management, negotiation, and organization of *individual congregations.* He also worked at building *a consciousness of unity, fellowship, and interdependency throughout the whole emerging Christian network.* This phenomenon is beautifully reflected in the special collection he promotes among the churches of Achaia and Macedonia for the needs of the church at Jerusalem. (See Acts 19:21-22; Rom. 15:25-27; 1 Cor. 16:1-4; 2 Cor. 8, 9).

It is not clear just what difficulties brought on the poverty in Jerusalem. The significant thing is that the need provides an opportunity for Paul to underscore and consolidate the new humanity which God is creating in the Christian community. This new humanity transcends all the old boundaries that separated Jews and Gentiles, Asians and Europeans, from one another in the world. "No longer do we distinguish between Greek and Jew, circumcised and uncircumcised, barbarian, Scythian, slave, free man, but Christ is all, and in all" (Col. 3:11; cf Gal. 3:28). Separate in every way in terms of prior identities and cultural heritage, Jews and Gentiles were now united in a new and decisive way through Christ. And this unity called them to transcultural responsibility for the well-being of one another.

All this, says Paul in Ephesians, results from the purpose of God "to unite all things in Christ (1:10). In Christ and his church God reconciles all people "in one body . . . thereby bringing hostility to and end" (2:16). No longer are any "strangers and sojourners" for all have been accepted into the new family of God (2:19). It is this new family which begins to become visible in the story of the New Testament.

" . . . *no longer do we distinguish between Greek and Jew, circumcised and uncircumcised, barbarian and Scythian, slave and free.*"

Chapter 5

Domestic Squabbles and Family Splits

It is typical of the paradox of the life of the church, in its double character as the divinely constituted Body of Christ, and at the same time a human assemblage of very imperfect men and women, that the writer to the Ephesians having, in the first part of his Epistle, in passage after passage of profound theology, laid the doctrinal foundation of the church's unity, proceeds in the second part to recognize the possibility of division within that Body. He warns his readers (4:31) against bitterness, wrath, anger, clamour, railing, and malice—the characteristic causes and expressions of division. The unity of the church is indeed divinely given, but it is a gift which must never be taken for granted. It must be striven for and enthusiastically safeguarded; otherwise it may be lost. The Epistle thus expresses in advance the apparent contradiction which runs through all Christian history and is the connecting thread in the history of the ecumenical movement—a recognition of that essential unity of all Christ's people, which though often obscured is never wholly lost; and the ever-repeated development of misunderstanding, contention, and division within the one fellowship. From this contradiction the church was not free even in the period of the New Testament.

(*A History of the Ecumenical Movement,* Ruth Rouse and Stephen Neill, p. 5.)

From the time of Jesus, who himself used the metaphor, it has been popular to use the analogy of marriage to describe the church. One could thus compare tha status of church unity in the latter half of the first century to the first year of newlyweds. The bride and groom discover, sometimes rather abruptly, that the wooing and the honeymoon is over. The new twenty-four hour relationship between them brings with it adjustments to one another's weaker sides, as well as best sides, and occasional disagreements and compromises. Yet the marriage survives, because the initial bond is secure.

So it was that the church was forced to deal with internal divisions and quarrels very early in its life. Nearly every one of Paul's letters indicates some degree of dissension in the local church. The first major congregational crisis reported in the New Testament was spawned in Corinth, a city with access to major ports on the trade route between East and West. Corinth was perhaps the most cosmopolitan city of the ancient world and hence a gathering ground for "every conceivable wind and doctrine." Influenced by the atmosphere of license and unrestricted individual freedom that existed in Corinth, the church had split into several parties. Each party had adopted a name after a Christian leader, without the consent or knowledge of the leaders.

The "Paul Party" was probably made up of Gentiles who interpreted Christian freedom as the license to do as one pleased. The "Apollos Party," named after an eloquent Alexandrian Jew, probably represented the philosophers in the church who sought to intellectualize Christianity. The "Cephas Party" probably consisted of traditionalist Jews in the group, who wanted more

" . . . the church was forced to deal with internal division and quarrels very early in its life."

legalism incorporated in the new religion. And the "Christ Party" was probably a collection of others who were not previously identified with any group or religion, but who were now so caught up in Christianity that they were self-righteously identifying with Christ, as if to say they were the only true Christians in Corinth.

The factions in Corinth were sparking so many problems and conflicts that Paul is literally beside himself with anxiety when he hears about them. The Judaizers (those who wanted more legalism and Jewish tradition) were attacking the apostle's credentials, claiming that since Paul was not one of the original twelve disciples, he was not qualified to direct Christian behavior. (2 Cor. 11). The Gentiles were claiming to be Christian while still engaging in illicit sexual habits (1 Cor. 5:1-2) and turning the love feast into a drinking party (1 Cor. 11:17-22). The intellectualizers were becoming so adept in Christian philosophy that they were ignoring Christian responsibility (1 Cor. 8). And the whole church needed a lesson in love for one another (which Paul so beautifully and perceptively provided in 1 Cor. 13).

There were additional examples of disunity in other mission churches of the first century. Two women in Philippi, Euodias and Syntyche, were disrupting the peace of their church with their personal incompatability. The church at Colossae appears to have had a heretical strain within it which wanted to belittle the authority of Christ. This may have been the first indication of a heresy later identified as Gnosticism, which held that all matter is evil, that only spirit can be good. This meant that the human side of Jesus was completely denied, and the human body wholly evil, both of which are ideas foreign to Jesus' own teaching.

Of lesser consequence was a twist of Christian freedom in Thessalonica, where a segment of the church was using Paul's teaching about the imminence of the second coming as an excuse to loaf and indulge on someone else's groceries (2 Th. 3:6-13). Such idleness definitely had a dis-unifying effect, for others took equally seriously the admonition to be evangelically zealous until the end came. The latter were not happy about those brothers and sisters who were nothing but moochers.

But the major threat to the new Christian movement, and which provided Paul his most trying moments, was the controversy over whether Gentiles could become Christians without circumcision. See Acts 15, and the whole letter of Galatians. What made it so formidable a controversy was that Paul's opposition was being led by the apostle James, the Elder at Jerusalem, who was also influencing Peter (Acts 21:17-21). Although Acts 15:12-35 reports a partial resolution of the controversy, advocates of circumcision continued to stir up unrest in churches such as those in Galatia.

Even when circumcision was not a formal requirement for Gentiles, relationships between Jews and Gentiles could be strained. In Antioch James' emissaries had arranged for two separate love feasts, one for the circumcised and one for the uncircumcised, and persuaded Peter to eat with the Jewish group. Since the breaking of bread was at the very heart of Christian unity, Paul's dander was raised (Gal. 2:9-14).

As serious as the controversy was, it had to do with differences within the family, not rival organizations:

> The strained and twisted style of the Epistle to the Galatians reveals to us something of the intensity of the conflicts of long ago. Yet these tensions were still felt to be in the nature of family quarrels; they were divisions of view and practice within the church, they were not yet divisions *of* the church or schisms *from* it. Paul in prison at Rome can rejoice over the preaching of his opponents, since, even though their motives may be questionable in one way or another Christ is being preached and that is the principal thing (Phil. 1:15-18). Fellowship may have been strained, but it had not been wholly destroyed.

(Rouse and Neill, *History of the Ecumenical Movement,* p. 6)

As the family grew larger and "adopted" members from various cultures and philosophies, and as the gap between Pentecost and the contemporary period widened, doctrinal disputes and heresies also increased. In addition to Gnosticism there developed in the first five centuries major controversies over the role of Christians in the world and the true nature of Christ.

The debate over Christians and the world was stirred up by the Montanists in the second century, the Novationists in the third, and the Donatists in the fourth century. They represented Christians who were disappointed that the church settled down to a rather routine style of life when the second coming of Christ did not take place in the first century as expected. They continually sought to revive the early enthusiasm for the "watch" and refused to be occupied with the mundane ministrations of the church.

The other controversy was by far the most sweeping of the early disagreements. A widespread debate flared c. A.D. 320 over the nature of Christ, with the principal debaters being Arius and Alexander. Arius held that Christ was a human representation of God but in no way one with the Father in essence or eternity. Alexander, however, bishop of Alexandria, believed in Christ's full divinity. The dispute bitterly divided the eastern sector of the church, with bishops lining up on both sides of the issue. The Emperor Constantine, who had declared Christianity a legal religion in A.D. 313 in the hope that the prevalent religion would help unify the Empire, interceded in the controversy. To "settle" the debate, he called the first ecumenical council at Nicaea in A.D. 325, at government expense. The council voted with Alexander, affirming Christ to be of "one essence with the Father." When Arius and two bishops refused to sign the creed, Constantine promptly banished them.

But the controversy was merely shoved onto the back burner, where it simmered and flared for the next century and a quarter. The debate was carried on mainly in the East, for it was the Greek theologians who liked to speculate and philosophize. Of interest is a quote from Gregory of Nyssa on the status of the controversy in Constantinople in 381:

> The whole city is full of it, the squares, the market places, the cross-roads, the alleyways; old clothes men, money-changers, food sellers: they are all busy arguing. If you ask someone to give you change, he philosophizes about the Begotten and the Unbegotten; if you inquire about the price of a loaf, you are told by way of reply, that the Father is greater and the Son is inferior; if you ask 'Is my bath ready?' the attendant answers that the Son is made out of nothing.
>
> (Quoted by Barry Till, *The Churches' Search for Unity,* page 80.)

In spite of four ecumenical councils called between 325 and 451 to settle the issue, schisms resulted from this first major doctrinal dispute. There was another pattern emerging at this time which further affected the church's unity. With the legalization of Christianity came its relationship to the state and the privilege to own property and erect headquarters (i.e., church buildings). This meant that the unifying force in the church shifted from faith, worship, and an inner spirit, to organization.

In the course of the ecumenical councils a struggle began to take shape between the bishop of Rome and the bishop of Constantinople for the right to determine and declare the faith of the church. Aggravating the tension was the Latin contempt for the Greeks' penchant for arguing. The fact that the latter boasted of being theologians *par excellence* did nothing to smooth troubled waters.

As the rivalry deepened, the points of difference increased. Issues included the use of leavened or unleavened bread, whether or not clergy could marry, the use of icons in worship, and even the date for the celebration of Easter. Although the gap widened and tension was at its height in 1054, there was no formal separation of the East from the West until 1204. It was at this time that the Fourth Crusade, made up of Christian mercenaries recruited to continue the struggle to regain Jerusalem from the Moslems, was persuaded by a political aspirant to sack Constantinople. Western hatred of the Greeks was an added incentive. Constantinople, the greatest Christian city of the world, was raided by Christian swords and the sacred relics from its churches carried back to Western places of worship. It is a tragic chapter in church history, and certainly an incredible reversal of the unity with which the church began. It is a schism which has never been healed, although we are happy to note increasing dialogue between the Eastern Orthodox and the Western churches.

In Western Christendom the Middle Ages were a period of political struggle and doctrinal dizziness. Normative faith was fashioned according to the whims of whichever pope was in power. All divergent viewpoints— and there were many, including those of the Waldensians and John Wycliff—were branded heresy. Toward the end of the fourteenth century a temporary division rocked the Western world, as a rival pope to the one in Rome was crowned in Avignon.

Yet for all the restlessness and political manuevering, there was a rather remarkable degree of unity within the Western church during the Middle Ages. Under the popes, some of whom were outstanding leaders, the university was born to provide unity in thought for the Holy Roman Empire. Latin was introduced for all the liturgy of the West. And there was, with one exception of the forty years of rival popes. no uncertainty about the center of authority in the church. From the standpoint of thought, worship, and authority, Christianity in the West was one.

But the glue was all on the outside—organizational and intellectual. There was little inward substance in the church, and little or no effort by the leaders to effect reform. It took a humble monk, who could not keep quiet about his personal experience with the Bible, to ignite the spark of reform. Martin Luther did not intend for his 95 theses to lead to anything more than a reawakening to biblical values in his own church. But his boldness was contagious and spread quickly, too quickly for Rome to call a reforming council. The break in the church's unity had been made and the flood gates opened.

Lutheranism not only blossomed in Germany but almost immediately spread north to Scandanavia. Simultaneously, Zwingli led the reform in Switzerland. By the time John Calvin began adding his influence to the movement, c. 1538, a bitter rivalry between the Roman Catholics and the Protestants was already raging, and the Roman Church was mounting a counter-attack. All sense of unity within the body of Jesus Christ had been shattered.

Even before the Reformation, there was another quiet revolution leading toward further schism. It too was born out of a hunger for simple, personal faith with no authority other than God's word. Two strains of reform evolved from this movement—the Anabaptist and the Pietist. From these two came the free and personal communions we know as the Baptists, Brethren, Mennonites, and Quakers.

Today's church reflects this long history of domestic squabbles and family splits. A young man was asked by a clergyman what church he preferred. "That's a good question," came the reply. "My father was Lutheran and my mother was Methodist, and since neither of them went to church I attended my step-grandmother's Baptist Church. But neither of my parents would let me join. When I was in college I occasionally went to the nearby Presbyterian Church. Then I married a Catholic girl and don't understand a thing about her church. So I guess you'd say I'm lost!"

This young man's situation may be more composite than most, but chances are he's not the only one who has found himself lost in the maze of Christian communions. According to the 1976 Britannica Book of the Year there are 954,766,700 Christians in the world, or approximately 25% of the earth's population. But they are divided as follows: 540,704,000 Roman Catholics, 327,509,100 Protestants, and 86,653,600 Eastern Orthodox. Furthermore, there are various branches and orders of Roman Catholicism; eight groups of Orthodox Christians; and 250 Protestant denominations. And there is a wide divergence in form of organization and sacraments, ethical teaching, and worship expression.

The question all this poses is clear: How can God's divided family rediscover the vision of unity which called it into being?

Chapter 6

Bridging the Gaps

"Physician, heal thyself."

It is to the eternal credit of the church that there have always been efforts from within to heal its divisions and settle its squabbles. We have already seen how Paul acted quickly and persistently to confront opposing parties within the early church. The Council of Jerusalem described in Acts 15, which met to decide the question of circumcision for Gentiles, may well be the first instance of calling together a representative body of Christian groups to reach consensus on doctrine and deed.

But we have also seen that Paul dealt *personally* with conflicts in the churches he established, the most notable example being the problems at Corinth. In the letters to the Corinthians we see how much peace and harmony within the church meant to Paul. He literally bears the problems of the Corinthians on his heart. Paul pours out every known emotion in his appeal to them to reconcile their differences. Apparently he even interrupts his own preplanned missionary schedule to visit them and be an on-the-scene mediator. Paul's pastoral concern for unity is caught up well in the closing words of 2 Corinthians:

> Finally, brethren, farewell.
>
> Mend your ways, heed my appeal, agree with one another, live in peace, and the God of love and peace will be with you. *Greet one another with a holy kiss.* All the saints greet you.
>
> The grace of the Lord Jesus Christ and the love of God and the fellowship of the Holy Spirit be with you *all.*
>
> (2 Corinthians 13:11-14)

It is safe to say that the primary glue that held the church together during its first centuries was the handing on of apostolic tradition, that is, the witness of the apostles to the meaning of the life, death, and resurrection of Jesus Christ. Paul rests his case to the Corinthians on this very point:

> For I delivered to you as of first importance what I also received, that Christ died for our sins in accordance with the scriptures, that he was buried, that he was raised on the third day in accordance with the scriptures, and that he appeared to Cephas, then to the twelve.
>
> (1 Corinthians 15:3-5)

In similar fashion, some of the early church patriarchs stress that their teaching is not their own but what they learned from the elders. (These were either the disciples or younger men who had had the privilige of sitting at the feet of the disciples.)

It was necessary, however, as time created a larger gulf between those who were contemporaries with Jesus and those who came after, to institute some tangible means of insuring unity and defending against heresy. One way was through the gathering of the *apostolic writings.* These apparently were collected by A.D. 180, even though they were not canonized as the New Testament until 400. Concurrent with the preservation of the apostles' writings was the development of a *creed,* probably to defend against Gnosticism. The earliest form of the so-called "Apostles' Creed" originated between 150 and 175 in Rome. The *sacraments* were also an important part of the early church's identity. Baptism was a rite of initiation into the body of Christ, and the eucharist was a renewal of Christian loyalty. A fourth visible means of maintaining unity and authenticity was the development of *organization,* specifically in a ministerial order.

In spite of these efforts, serious doctrinal differences still arose, resulting in part from geographical separation. To deal with these disputes the bishops of the various local churches were called together in ecumenical councils. We have already noted the first of these, the Council of Nicaea called by Emperor Constantine in 325. The next three hundred years saw six more of these major attempts to smooth differences within the church. The councils were only partially successful, for they almost all had interference or direction by the state. This virtually assured dilution of the faith. But they were at least an attempt within the church to doctor its own wounds and restore its wholeness.

There were many who were hoping for a council that would prevent the split at the time of the Protestant Reformation. But the established church could not get in gear for such until 1545 (the Council of Trent), twenty-eight years after Martin Luther's dynamic poster. By then the revolution was rolling with a full head of steam, and the council was used to form the Roman Church's defense.

Meanwhile, the Protestants were having their own squabbles and divisions. For example, the Germans and the Swiss could not agree on how to celebrate communion. Several councils were called to try to reach agreement. It is interesting that the leading Protestant proponents of ecumenicity during the Reformation period were laymen, particularly men who had traveled and had had contact with persons of other communions. Their principal means of promoting unity was writings, in which they attacked the folly of exclusiveness and advocated unity in order for the church to achieve good in the world. Unfortunately, they were ahead of their time.

No century of church history has been without a representative conscience that acted as a vanguard for unity. The modern ecumenical movement dates to 1910, but the nineteenth century had a number of important antecedents. With the expansion of Christianity to America denominations began to add world conferences to their program of activity. Although these were not interfaith, they did deal with ecumenical issues. In America, itself, there was Plan of Union between the Presbyterians and the Congregationalists between 1801 and 1852 for the purposes of a stronger evangelistic appeal. In the same century there were conversations toward unity between the Lutherans and the Reformed churches. The outcome of these and similar relationships was the formation of the Federal Council of Churches in America in 1908, the forerunner of the modern National Council of Churches in the USA. The Federal Council was not specifically intended for organic unity, but to provide a forum for ecumenical discussion.

The nineteenth century in England produced another kind of ecumenical venture. It was here that the YMCA and the Student Christian Movement began, composed of members from several faiths, but operated apart from ecclesiastical tradition and rules. These organizations had a profound effect upon later ecumenical effort, because Christians discovered that they *could* work together. And some of the later leaders of the more notable ecumenical activity were products of the Student Christian Movement.

Another nineteenth century European impetus to the modern ecumenical movement was the sudden development of missionary activity. As various communions dispatched missionaries to foreign countries, the workers soon discovered that it was both healthier and supportive

" ... no century of church history has been without ... a vanguard for unity."

to cooperate with one another. The push was on to call an interdenominational missionary council to discuss cooperative and common strategy.

In 1910 the first such venture took place at Edinburgh, Scotland, with 1200 delegates from 159 denominational missionary societies. The leadership for the Edinburgh Council consisted of young men who could devote many valuable remaining years of their lives to church unity: John R. Mott, William Temple, John Baillie, Charles Henry Brent. Three things were significant about this gathering: (1) It was interdenominational. (2) It was concerned with the mission of the church, a fundamental reason for unity. (3) It established an International Missions Committee to continue the cooperative effort it had started. The International Missions Committee laid the foundation for local ecumenicity, as it established branches called "National Missions Councils" all over the world. The Edinburgh Council had established one clear thing: It was possible to at least call the church together for conversation.

Fifteen years and one world war later, Archbishop Söderblom of Sweden conceived a plan to bring Christians together to talk about the role of the church in social, international and industrial problems. The effort was labeled the "Life and Work Movement." The first conference, in 1925, brought together 1,000 representatives from thirty-seven countries. These included, for the first time in an ecumenical meeting for 500 years, delegates from the Eastern Orthodox Churches.

Bishop Charles Henry Brent, one of the Edinburgh leaders, was not happy that the ecumenical meetings were dealing only with external matters. He wanted to get at the heart of disunity: the differences in doctrine and devotional practice. Soon after the Life and Work Conference, Bishop Brent headed a delegation that toured the European churches in an attempt to drum up interest in a

"Faith and Order Movement." Although he struck out in his bid with the Germans and with the Roman Catholics, he still generated enough interest to hold a conference at Lausanne in 1927. The first effort only succeeded in revealing how pronounced the differences had become. But at least a committee for continuing dialogue was established, and a second conference in 1937 produced a united statement on the meaning of the phrase, often used in prayers, "the grace of our Lord Jesus Christ."

Another significant attempt at ecumenical understanding was initiated by the Anglican Church in 1920. At the Lambeth Conference the Church of England called for worldwide Christian unity. Though it concluded that the Episcopate was the one true way to bring the church together, it softened the Anglicans toward further ecumenical cooperation and gave an important impetus to the emerging efforts.

With the Life and Work Movement, the Faith and Order Movement, the International Missionary Council, the Lambeth Conference, and the World Sunday School Association among other alliances all working toward restoring some semblance of Christian unity, there was a mighty cloud gathering from many coverging winds. Abetting the process was the increasing cross-sharing of the churches' scholars in exploring the great themes of the Bible.

The time was ripe to bring all of these ecumenical ventures and movements under one umbrella. In 1938 representatives of the Life and Work and Faith and Order movements, elected by 130 interested churches, voted to merge and form the World Council of Churches. The constitution drafted defined the Council simply as "a fellowship of churches which accept our Lord Jesus Christ as God and Savior." It emphasized that the Council was in no way to legislate for its member communions. A Provisional Committee was established to formally organize the Council, unaware that its efforts were soon to be hampered by the outbreak of World War II.

Nevertheless, by the time the war started, fifty churches had accepted membership in the World Council, a number that grew to ninety by 1945 and reached 286 churches from ninety different countries by 1976. In 1961, at the Third Assembly of the Council, the basis for membership was expanded to read: "The World Council of Churches is a fellowship of churches which confess the Lord Jesus Christ as God and Savior according to the Scriptures and therefore seek to fulfill their common calling to the glory of the one God, Father, Son and Holy Spirit."

The themes of the world assemblies of the WCC reflect points at which the Council has successfully shared meaningful dialogue: "Man's Disorder and God's Design" (Amsterdam, 1948), "Jesus Christ, the Hope of the World" (Evanston, 1954), "Jesus Christ the Light of the World" (New Delhi, 1961), "Behold, I Make All Things New" (Uppsala, 1968), "Jesus Frees and Unites" (Nairobi, 1975). Much creative theological discussion has taken place within the meetings of the Faith and Order and Life and Work Committees (the latter renamed "Church and Society"), which meet between the world assemblies. Increasingly the committees are becoming aware that "faith" and "works" are interrelated, and dialogue between the two groups indicates another step toward unity.

In addition to its Division of Studies, the WCC exercises two other vital functions: (1) It has served as a channel of aid, both to churches in distress and for the relief of human suffering or the improvement of social conditions. Particularly significant has been the Council's ministry among refugees and in areas stricken by natural disasters. (2) Working closely with the United Nations and other international humanitarian agencies, the WCC has shared its concern over such world issues as human rights, economic and social development, racism, world justice, and most recently, peace and non-violence.

While much anxiety and dissatisfaction has been expressed both within and beyond the WCC regarding its success as a cooperative venture, there is little doubt that its overarching witness has made an impact upon Christendom. One example is the union of the Church of South India which was consummated in 1947. The Church of South India (C.S.I.) brought together four very different denominations: Presbyterians, Congregationalists, Methodists, and the South India dioceses of the Anglican Church of India, Burma and Ceylon. There were some organizational and sacramental differences to iron out at first, but in recent years the C.S.I. has demonstrated that differing traditions are capable of uniting in organization and worship.

C.S.I. was the first of a number of church unions negotiated around the world. Churches in northern India formed the Church of North India in 1970, with six denominations entering the united church. In 1965 four denominations in Ecuador formed the United Evangelical Church. In the late sixties the churches of Nigeria began a closer cooperation which led to a federation called the Churches of Christ in Sudan. Australia and New Zealand, Japan, England, and Ghana are other countries in which there are serious discussions of unity among national churches. The World Council's journal *Ecumenical Review,* Volume 28, No. 3, July 1976, lists 29 countries in which church union negotiations have been noted between 1973 and 1975.

In the United States, a number of denominational mergers have been consummated in the twentieth century. One of the most heralded was that uniting the Evangelical United Brethren with the Methodist Church, creating the United Methodist denomination. Even more ambitious have been the efforts of six major Protestant denominations in the U.S. to form one new church "truly catholic, truly reformed, and truly evangelical." Together these six communions would combine a membership of 22 million members, approximately one-third of the total Protestant population in the United States. Formerly known as the Consultation on Church Union, it is now referred to as the Church of Christ Uniting. Other communions were invited to join in the effort or to send observers who could contribute toward the plan for union. Largely the work of denominational leaders up to this point, COCU is only now being explored at the grassroots level in individual congregations. There, progress is slow.

National councils of churches function much like the WCC, but on the national and regional level. The National Council of Churches in the USA provides a forum and a united stance on national issues for thirty-one Protestant communions. It also administers through Church World Service a program of relief and emergency help that extends around the world. Many educational and evangelistic aids are produced for use by member churches. The National Association of Evangelicals, established in 1944, is a federation of Protestant denominations with a more conservative, evangelical approach. The NAE stresses missionary witness and adheres to biblical directives in life and faith.

Obvious in this survey of ecumenical effort spanning the four and one half centuries since the Protestant Reformation is the absence of Roman Catholic membership. The Eastern Orthodox Church is now a part of the WCC, but so far Rome has not made a move to join, although the way has been open. That is not to say that progress has been nil in restoring relationships between Protestants and Roman Catholics. While it has not happened on the world scene, many national and local councils of churches now have Roman Catholic members, and there is much more dialogue and shared worship between the two main streams of Christianity.

The new openness and relationship can be attributed in large part to Vatican II (1962-65), a meeting of the Council of Cardinals convened by Pope John XXVIII in 1962 and continued under his successor, Paul VI. The major conclave was not summoned to deal primarily with the Roman Church's relations with other churches. But in the participants' struggles with the nature and purpose of their church, the authenticity of other groups within Christendom was officially recognized. Catholics were subsequently urged to associate with other brethren and to seek areas of common work and agreement.

Vatican II has inspired and opened the way for several significant joint efforts between Catholics and Protestants, including "Living Room Dialogues" in many communities. These are small group encounters between laypersons of the two communions designed to improve understanding. The emphasis of the Vatican upon restoring dialogue has increased awareness and use of the Week of Prayer for Christian Unity (always January 18-25), which was actually conceived in 1935 by Friar Paul Couturier.

None of the efforts described in this session has been a panacea to the divisions within Christendom. But each has contributed significantly to bridging the gap and bringing Christians into closer fellowship with one another in the name of their one Lord, Jesus Christ.

Chapter 7

New Accents
in Ecumenical Conversations

The 1970's have introduced a world with a character uniquely different from any other period in the history of civilization. Human knowledge has increased and spread so rapidly since the midpoint of the century, that the resulting changes in the global community have been staggering to the sociological mind. It would be well for us to review some of the characteristics of this world within which we live, before examining how the ecumenical movement is responding to the change.

One of the most visible manifestations of the "new world" of the seventies is the effect of space exploration. The achievements in the space program, especially the conquest of the moon, have restored a spirit of Renaissance and humanism, a new confidence in human ability. Space station relay satellites have enabled the average person to sit in the comfort of one's easy chair and watch the news *as it happens* on the opposite side of the globe. "Instant replay" has helped us test the validity of our own perceptions. Space technology has thus heightened awareness of the co-existence of all people and the way we are dependent upon one another.

A second phenomenon of the new age has been the emergence of independent nations. In the past thirty years nearly 100 new nations have been formed, representing the majority of humankind. Most of these were previously territorial states on the continents of Africa and Asia. Under young and often Western-educated indigenous leadership, the old colonial bonds have been successfully broken. Not only has this broadened the base of the human family. It has also increased the number of world neighbors to and for whom we are accountable. Additionally, it has established credibility for people of different races and in previously remote places. They are no longer to be regarded as inferior in intelligence, civilization, and the ability to be autonomous.

Along with the emergence of the so-called "Third World" has come, third, a new spirit of freedom and independence among previously subservient or oppressed groups. These include the feminist movement, student bodies, black coalitions, etc. As these groups have affirmed their identity, they have challenged old ways of relating to one another and made experimental personal and social roles both possible and more urgent.

A fourth major concern of the seventies has been the crisis of diminishing natural resources and abuse of the environment. Adding to the crisis is the fact that the world's population is rapidly increasing and that people are living longer. These realities have led to a heightened awareness of human need, as well as to a new emphasis upon the global community. It has challenged responsible individuals, nations, and groups to speak to the problems of world hunger and the stewardship of energy-producing resources.

Fifth, the current era in the United States has been one

of economic crises. There has been a constant struggle for the seat of power between corporations and governmental agencies (although at times the distinction is not nearly that clear). Inflation and unemployment have hit new peacetime highs. Rising costs have made additional hardships for the poor and restricted the programs of many churches. But both corporations and the Congress have remained aloof from those affected. There is a sense of futility in the financial future for many groups.

Sixth, the prevailing moral climate is marked by a breaking down of the taboos of earlier days. There is generally more acceptance of unqualified abortion, premarital or non-conventional living together, and homosexual coping. Relatively unchallenged is the common use of obscenity, sex, and violence on television, stage and screen, as well as in the written media. Much activity that is perpetuated or condoned by modern governments or industrial giants is designed to accomplish political or economic gain through the exploitation of classes or groups of people. Ours is an era in which many of the eighteenth and nineteenth "purist" restraints upon human behavior have been abandoned (or defied).

It is not difficult to sense the challenge to the church in a world such as we have described. The gospel is relevant to all of life. And the purpose of the church is to be the agent of God's blessing to *all the nations* and families of the earth. The church *must* make its witness today, *and a united witness which is significant enough to command attention.*

Realizing this imperative task, the World Council of Churches assembled at Nairobi sharpened the aim of the Council by amending its constitutional phrases on unity to read: "visible unity in one faith and one eucharistic fellowship, expressed in worship and in common life in Christ, in order that the world may believe." The key words are "visible unity." What does visible unity mean?

John Deschner, speaking before a plenary session at Nairobi, expressed it this way:

> Visible unity is challenging, dangerous, promising. It challenges "cheap ecumenism," superstructure ecumenism, which will give to the cause of church unity fellowship, delegates, cooperation, even money, but not visible local change. But it is also dangerous, for it can tempt us to think that what needs to become visible is merely the merger of church organizations. No, what needs to become visible is a witness which embodies among Christians and Christian churches a believable sign of the liberating unity-in-controversy which God has promised to all humankind.
>
> (*The Ecumenical Review*, WCC, Vol. 28, No. 1, January 1976, p. 22)

Professor Deschner points to the predominant trend of current ecumenical thought, which has been described as "conciliarity." The new concept of conciliarity should not be confused with conciliar movements or councils of churches. The concept is bigger than either merger or federation. It takes into account and approves of organic, denominational union. But it is much more seriously concerned about authentic experiences and forms of unity at the local congregational level.

Conciliarity is manifest in the mutual recognition of members and ministers, full communion, mutual help, and common action. But it does not require one common form of church government, worship, or custom. It is possible to maintain the integrity of the apostolic faith and proclaim it in unison without ascribing to a uniform polity, rite, or even creed. Conciliarity recognizes that there are differing forms of expression and that these will and can remain in the one church of Jesus Christ on earth.

The new trend in ecumenism has several definitive characteristics:

(1) A transcending of *denominationalism*. While recognizing that denominations provide the structure by which the various communions of Christendom are identified, the new unity looks beyond the supposed

denominational boundaries. It affirms the ministries that can be done together or as a service to one another. Denominations are no longer seen as rivals in competition with one another but as complementary "brothers" and "sisters" in the mission of the whole family.

(2) *More emphasis upon joint action and less on doctrinal consensus.* The purpose for unity is not so much to establish the church as to be a dynamic power for the reconciliation of all in God's kingdom. The church's unity serves as a leaven in humanity to deliver the dream of Christ's mission: "Preach good news to the poor, proclaim release to the captives, restore sight to the blind, set at liberty those who are oppressed, proclaim the acceptable year of the Lord" (Luke 4:18-19). Thus, more important than whether denominations can agree on the ultimate form of salvation is the need for an inclusive world community. This community will include all kinds and sorts of persons, not only Christians, or Brethren, but the poor and forsaken, the handicapped, the minorities, the elderly, the oppressed—and on and on across all human conditions.

(3) *Recognition of the validity of indigenous churches, churches related to the culture of the people and administered by native leadership.* This represents a new acceptance of the faith and capability of all of the family. Paternalism by arrogant and self-righteous nations is no longer tolerated. There is a growing appreciation for the faith perspectives that different cultures can give to the gospel message, and concurrently a different perspective on the validity of unity within diversity.

(4) *A shift from regional, national, and international emphases to that of unity on the local scene.* This is seen in the local cluster (three or more congregations of various communions in geographical proximity, practicing conciliarity) and in interfaith study and worship. It is at the grass roots that a genuine feeling of fam-

" . . . (there is) a new acceptance of the faith and capability of all of the family."

ily kinship, of unity within diversity, can be fostered.

(5) *More involvement by the church as a catalyst for community.* There is a greater degree of willingness on the part of the church to be the enabler and support for total community action. The churches are working with community residents on their needs for adequate housing, a cleaner and safer neighborhood, medical and material aid, and quality education and human rights. It is encouraging evidence that congregations and communions are breaking out of narrow parochialism and accepting the role of reconcilers of humanity.

(6) *Less defensiveness.* We noted earlier the trend toward conciliarity, removing the pressure to merge organic structures. Coupled with the challenge to the church from the secular world, this has eased the sense of competitiveness and the tendency toward defensiveness among denominations. There does appear to be a new air of tolerance and congeniality, at least among the communions in the mainstream of Protestantism and Catholicism. John Deschner identifies "hospitality" as being a crucial aspect of authentic conciliar fellowship. Citing the Council at Jerusalem in Acts 15, he spells it out this way:

> When the Antioch delegates arrive, they are "welcomed" by the church and the apostles and the elders in Jerusalem. I sometimes think that the whole ecumenical problem and hope can be summed up in the word "hospitality." They are welcomed, not merely as tired travellers, or merely as old friends, but recognized and welcomed as authorized representatives of a controversial sister church. An important detail: They are recognized in their diversity; Titus, an uncircumcized Greek, is also fully recognized and welcomed (Gal. 2:5). Moreover—for this gives the meeting its seriousness—they are fully recognized as representative spokesmen for the whole Church, whose controversial mission in the profoundest sense belongs to both the Jerusalem and the Antioch churches. That is the meaning of the right hand of fellowship.

> *(Ibid., p. 24)*

(7) *Reaffirmation of the church's relevance.* There is

a new emphasis upon the word the church can proclaim in response to the world's problems. There is an attempt to restore a measure of authenticity and authority to the place of the church in the global society. As the World Council continues to include communions from additional nations in its membership, the influence of the church upon common human issues should become more of a reality. But even on the local scene there is an increased interest and involvement in community affairs.

With these various new accents, ecumenism takes seriously the changing world we spoke of earlier. It recognizes the need to work at unity in the church in the context of the struggles and aspirations of the whole human family.

Chapter 8

We Too Are Part of the Story

The Church of the Brethren today is a full-fledged participant in the ecumenical movement. Its spirit of cooperation and fraternal relations took nearly two hundred years to develop, however. The denomination was conceived out of a protest against the practices of the established churches of 18th century Europe. By virtue of their illegality, the early Brethren were forced to develop sectarian defenses, which they carried with them to the new world. They liked what they had, and to retain it they were willing to endure imprisonment, punishment, uprooting from their homes, a long, hard ocean voyage, and finally, a raw wilderness to conquer in Penn's Woods. They naturally stuck together, and no doubt during those difficult years of early Pennsylvania they needed the close-knit support of each other to survive the discouragement and hardship.

In 1742 Count Zinzendorf, a Moravian, sought to organize the Germanic religious groups of Pennsylvania

"... we too are part of the story."

into a union under the motto: "In essentials unity, in non-essentials diversity, in all things charity." An invitation was extended to the Brethren, who attended several of the prelimianry synods called to work out grounds of unity. But the Brethren did not like the Count's desire to evangelize the Indians using the sprinkling mode of baptism. They were also suspicious that Zinzendorf wanted to make tham all Moravians. The Brethren withdrew indignantly and decided to bolster their defense by holding their own Great Council in 1742, the forerunner of the denomination's Annual Conference.

The years between 1750 and 1860 have sometimes been referred to as the Dark Ages in the life of the Brethren. Until recently there were very few records of Brethren activity for this period available. Brethren historians Don Durnbaugh and Roger Sapington have industriously uncovered some vital material to enlighten the dearth. (See in particular *The Brethren in the New Nation,* a source book by Roger Sappington on Brethren during the years 1785-1860, published by The Brethren Press. The section "Relations With Other Religious Groups," pp. 103-122, relates directly to our discussion here.)

The Brethren during those years maintained some notable fraternal relationships with four groups: the Mennonites, with whom they shared peace concerns; the Brethren in Christ, who came to the Brethren for help in organizing; the Universalists, whose views were apparently compatible enough with those of the Brethren to justify frequent "pulpit exchanges"; and the Disciples, with whom the Brethren debated merger for many years. In fact, the leaders of the Brethren, Disciples, and occasionally the Baptists, engaged in frequent debates during the period regarding the true salvation. Of course, each group claimed to possess the only answer!

Most embarrassing during the nineteenth century Brethren history are the major schisms of 1881 and 1882, when the German Baptist Brethren Church was split into three camps: the Old Order, the Progressive Brethren, and the German Baptists. The precipitating issues were external matters. primarily how to deal with the new inventions and social customs accompanying the great American Industrial Revolution.

Along with many of its sister communions, the Church of the Brethren prepared the way for its participation in the modern ecumenical movement through the foreign mission program. In 1894 the first Brethren missionaries to India were encouraged to cooperate closely with other missionaries and to observe the principle of comity. Concurrently, on the home front, the Brethren were already using the interdenominational International Sunday School Lessons, publishing the first continuing Brethren quarterly in 1886.

In 1904 a fraternal delegate from the Progressive Brethren addressed Annual Conference Standing Committee. And in 1910 W. J. McNight of the Reformed Presbyterian Church of North America delivered greetings from his communion to Annual Conference. The first committee to receive fraternal communications from other groups was appointed by Standing Committee in 1914. And in 1916 an inquiry was made regarding Brethren membership in the Federal Council of Churches.

With the outbreak of World War I, the Brethren, Friends, and Mennonites developed some cooperation in witnessing to their common peace concerns. Immediately following the war, Brethren leaders joined the bandwagon of Protestant churches who were going to start the Interchurch World Movement. The boards of the denomination had already committed Brethren funds for the project when Annual Conference refused to ratify participation and required the boards to withdraw. The movement collapsed soon afterward, and this fiasco did not enhance the image of ecumenical relations for many of the Brethren.

However, in 1925 two congregations, one from Idaho and one from Western Pennsylvania, sent queries to Annual Conference requesting appointment of a committee to study the possible reuniting of the Church of the Brethren and the Brethren (Progressive) Church. Three years later J. W. Lear made an epoch-setting statement before the denomination's Council of Boards, in which he began with the observation, "The order given by Christ to His Church is much too large for our small denomination to undertake alone." (See Appendix 2 for the full statement.)

These events paved the way for the appointment of a permanent Fraternal Relations Committee in 1934, and the appointment of M. R. Zigler as the representative to the Oxford Conference on Life and Work and the Edinburgh Conference on Faith and Order, both in 1937. Four years later Annual Conference approved by a very large majority vote our joining the Federal Council of Churches. Since that time the denomination has consistently sent a full complement of delegates to the World Council assemblies and to the meetings of the National Council of Churches, the successor to the Federal Council.

Augmenting Brethren participation in the organization of ecumenical activity have been the contributions of many Brethren individuals. The dean of Brethren ecumenists has to be M. R. Zigler, whose strong peace witness and humanitarian interests were frequently heard by the World Council. Zigler also headed the Brethren program of relief and rehabilitation in Europe following World War II and served concurrently as the liaison with the World Council of Churches office in Geneva. Zigler's efforts gained him a seat on the Central Committee of the World Council, on which he served until 1961. Norman J. Baugher, former executive secretary of the General Board of the Church of the Brethren, also served on the Central Committee, from 1961 to 1968. Warren F. Groff has served as a member of the World Council's Faith and Order Commission.

Since the National Council of Churches began in 1950, four Brethren have served as officers and ten others as members of the National Council staff. In addition, a number of Brethren have served as State Council of Churches executives and as members of the staffs of other conciliar organizations such as the Fellowship of Reconciliation, CROP, the National Service Board for Religious Objectors, Heifer Project (begun by Brethren Dan West) and Agricultural Missions, Inc. Most recently M. R. Zigler has given impetus to a new ecumenical venture called "On Earth Peace," to champion the biblical peace witness throughout the world. And the General Board has joined with a large group of denominations in addressing the gospel to the world hunger situation, the organization known as WHEAT.

Brethren overseas missions continued to work cooperatively with the leadership of other communions. Today Brethren congregations in India, Africa, and Ecuador are members of union churches: the Church of North India, the Church of South India, Ekklesiyar 'Yan'uwa a Nijeriya, and the United Evangelical Church in Ecuador.

One other unique link with a foreign communion has been an exchange of visits between the Brethren and the Russian Orthodox Church. This relationship grew out of the Russian Church's desire to be in dialogue with an American church concerned for peace, which culminated in a discussion between Brethren and Orthodox delegates to the 1961 WCC Assembly in New Delhi, India. Visits were exchanged in 1963 and 1967, the latter led by one of the top Russian Orthodox leaders, Metropolitan Nikodim. These were followed by two joint peace seminars. at Geneva in 1969, and at Kiev in 1971.

Yet another phase of Brethren ecumenical activity concerns the denomination's relationships to and conversations with other communions. The oldest such fraternalizing is that with the Brethren Church (Ashland), with whom ecumenical conversations have been maintained for forty years. While the two groups have never been able to agree to reunite, many successful cooperative ventures have taken place, notably joint historical research and sharing of information regarding common heritage.

Other bodies with whom conversations have existed through the period between 1940 and 1970 include the Mennonites, Quakers, Churches of God in North America, Church of God (Anderson), the Evangelical Free Church of North America, and the American Baptist Convention. With most of the groups the talks have been carried out at a committee level and have explored common interests and beliefs and possible ministries that could be done together. The Mennonites shared the facilities of Bethany Biblical Seminary during the years 1945-1958.

The nature of fraternal conversations took a new twist in 1972 when Annual Conference approved a proposal from the Committee on Interchurch Relations to enter into an "associated relationship" with the American Baptist Convention. The proposal did not call for a formal union or merger of the two bodies but for closer fellowship and cooperation at various levels of church life. Essentially the associated relationship has resulted in several cooperative services being shared by the two communions (rather than duplicating efforts), joint ministries, and even some congregational and district staff mergers.

The Church of the Brethren had a brief courtship with COCU (the Church of Christ Uniting) in the nineteen-sixties, during which observers were sent to the preliminary discussions of the proposed leviathan union. In 1965 a proposal was introduced before Annual Conference calling for full participation for the Brethren in the union. Perhaps nothing in this century has provoked more discussion and emotional outbursts on the floor of the annual meeting. The proposal was soundly defeated, but the reverberations were heard for several years afterward.

One area of interdenominational union that has found notable attraction among at least 2% of Brethren membership is the merger of two or more congregations of differing denominations within a given locale. In Virginia Beach, Virginia, for example, the Church of the Brethren and the United Church of Christ congregations have combined to provide a fellowship strong enough to sustain a pastor, provide a community ministry and build a modern church building. All members are made members of both denominations, and elements from both traditions go into each worship service. Forest Wells, pastor, says: "Neither Brethren nor UCC has given up anything. Rather, each is richer and fuller for having embraced one another's traditions. There was a time when I wondered if Christianity could transcend its differences. I don't make a push for all Christians uniting in one church, but we do need a model here and there."

Similarly united congregations combine Brethren and UCC members in Erie, Pennsylvania, and Brethren and American Baptists in Wenatchee, Washington. Freedom to experiment with worship and ecclesiastical form has been a joy for the Erie union. Denominational affiliation is not discussed at all when members are received. They are considered members of the body of Christ. The pastor, Levi Ziegler, holds ministerial ordination in both denominations. Albert Sauls, pastor of the Wenatchee Brethren-Baptist Church United, says the union has "forced us all to rethink what tradition and church membership means. We have challenged each other to bring out the best of one another's tradition."

All of the union congregations report the ability to be more evangelistic. The results both from the broader base of appeal and the quality of openness which the union suggests to the community.

Another different model of congregational union is the Southside Fellowship at Elkhart, Indiana, where members of the Church of the Brethren and two different bodies of Mennonites are affiliated. While the group has found it is impossible to completely transcend denominational identity, they have concentrated on trying to live the New Testament in their daily lives. Small support groups are the center of the church's fellowship. Lois Bare, the fellowship's administrative assistant and the only full-time staff member, says: "The church is my local point of contact with a whole great big body of Christians and where I can see Christ's body around the world embodied. My church is people whom I know and have contact with during the week. My small group really wants to live Jesus' way and know what Christ means." One problem she notes is the difficulty of interpreting to the children of the fellowship how they can be Mennonite and Brethren at the same time.

In 1968, as part of a major organizational change, Annual Conference replaced the Fraternal Relations Committee with a new Committee on Interchurch Relations, to be jointly constituted by Annual Conference and the General Board. The committee was to "carry forward current conversations and such other activities with other communions as will further the purpose of mutual understanding and the exploration of the question of church union" (*Minutes of the Annual Conferences of the Church of the Brethren,* 1965-1969, p. 338). The Committee has a part-time staff person to administer its work, DeWitt L. Miller. Warren F. Groff, president of Bethany Theological Seminary, serves as a theological advisor.

The Committee on Interchurch Relations has taken its task seriously and consistently struggled with an ecumenical stance for the Brethren that will represent the call and will of God for his church. Regular statements from the Committee to Annual Conference reflect this conscientious effort. Especially provocative are these words from their 1973 report:

> Ecumenicity requires of us that we 'give an account of the faith that is in us' before our brothers/sisters in the faith, and before the world. It is expected that we evidence specific ways that Christ in His Lordship is in fact being obeyed through the particular traditions from which we continue to draw strength. And we give an accounting before Christian groupings and our brothers/sisters in the larger human community around points of strength, from the very center of our life and work as a believing people. We do more than proliferate programs at the edges of our congregational consciousness. We affirm one another's strength, seeking to experience each other's tradition from inside as each particular history has mediated Christ in His Lordship.

The Committee on Interchurch Relations continues to search for the most effective means to express the denomination's relationship to the whole body of Christ.

Chapter 9

The Quest for Unity as a Brethren Calling

Which stance is more characteristically Brethren—sectarian or ecumenical? That is the question with which we shall deal in this session. Our answer will be guided by evidence within the denomination's faith perspective which strongly supports an ecumenical style.

We recognize at once, however, that the subject is controversial. The Fall 1975 issue of *Brethren Life and Thought* contained a symposium of opinions on this very subject, prompted by the thesis of Warren F. Groff's lead article that "the unity of the church is not in conflict with, but springs out of the very center of Brethren identity." Reactions to Dr. Groff's proposal that true Brethrenism is more catholic (i.e. universal) than clannish were definitely no more unified than Christendom itself.

A case can be made for labeling the Church of the Brethren provincial or sectarian. Its very size makes it suspicious (179,000 members in 1976). Its evangelism, confined during the first two hundred years to activity among only rural, German-speaking people, points up rather quickly the early exclusiveness of the church.

Evidence from 18th century documents shows that the original Brethren adopted a seemingly self-righteous attitude regarding the proper mode of baptism, which they believed to be immersion. Their intolerant insistence earned them the "stubborn separatists' award." George Adam Martin, writing in the Ephrata Chronicle, c. 1720 or 1721, says of the Brethren: "At the very commencement they adopted needless restrictions in that they did not allow anyone who was not baptized (by immersion) to partake with them of the holy sacrament. Had they not been so sectarian in this matter, and been more given to impartial love, they would have found entrance to more souls in their great awakening and noticeably promoted the glory of God" (cited by Donald Durnbaugh, *European Origins of the Brethren,* p. 295).

The tendency to lay claim to a certain divine "chosenness" has always been in evidence among the Brethren. It has surfaced in the pride often associated with its practice of non-conformity, in the cliqueishness of heredity that labels certain family names as distinctly and historically Brethren, and in the defensive guardianship of parochial customs and traditions. It was, furthermore, not until well into the twentieth century that membership in the denomination was open to persons not baptized by immersion without the requirement of rebaptism. Nor were such persons welcome at the love feast in earlier days. Brethren practiced the "ban" on through the 19th century, disfellowshipping any brother or sister who violated one of the church's convictions. At times such expulsion went to what seems now to be a rather harsh extreme. Persons received the plank for such "crimes" as a sister wearing a hat to church instead of the covering, and a man growing a mustache without a beard. Both were considered examples of worldliness!

One *could* argue from these historical examples that sectarianism is the predominant force behind Brethren existence. The evidence cited points to a group with barbed-wire boundaries, erected as much to keep the wolves out as to preserve the sheep within. It reveals a self-contented (if not self-righteous!) community, willing to make friends and fellow disciples only on its own terms. But is this the whole story?

A counter-case can be developed for the Brethren as ecumenists. Rick Gardner, in his *Brethren Life and Thought* response to Warren Groff's article writes: "Running deeper than any of these specific episodes of setting limits and boundaries is an interior momentum toward seeking unity and family togetherness that is an irrevocable part of our heritage."

Both Gardner and Groff are calling the church to examine some of the basic ingredients that make us who we are as a denomination. In doing so we discover that our theology—in other words, our understanding of God's will for us—definitely points us in the direction of unity rather than exclusiveness or parochialism. The "ecumenical" features of what might be called the "Brethren consciousness" include the following:

Family feeling. A young woman stood up in a morning worship service during a period of sharing to say: "The thing that thrills me most about being a part of the Church of the Brethren is the family feeling I get here. It's just like everybody is accepted as part of one big family. Everybody cares about everyone else." The speaker had been a member of the Brethren congregation for three years, having transferred from another denomination.

The woman was putting her finger on a vital clue to Brethren identity, not only a denominational lineage preserved through family names and intermarriages, but also a fellowship (koinonia) that carries a genuine sense of brotherhood (and sisterhood!) The family feeling is evident long after the postlude has dismissed the congregation from Sunday morning worship, as persons (sometimes by families) stand around sharing their joys and heartbreaks. The family feeling is preserved and celebrated on a larger scale in the denomination's Annual Conference, which functions more as a "family reunion" than as a governing agency.

The Brethren simply do not conceive of salvation apart from communal fellowship. Salvation is realized within the community of faith, where each cares for the other and each is accountable to the other in the name and spirit of Christ. The major rites of "family membership"— confession of faith, membership vows, baptism—take place most appropriately when the whole congregational family is present.

This commitment to a faith-in-community (as contrasted with a strongly individualistic religion) has led the Brethren to widen the family boundaries. We acknowledge an accountability to an extended family beyond the denomination, as seen in the ecumenical participation described in Session 8. In *Church of the Brethren Past and Present,* Vernard Eller relates that the Brethren "introduced the practice of open communion and transfer of membership by affirmation of faith ahead of some other denominations of their type" (p. 44).

It is also interesting that, according to Eller, the Brethren in recent years have recovered a doctrine, held by the original German Brethren, of the ultimate restoration of all humanity. Such an emphasis would be a natural outgrowth of the family model, for the genetic family ideally desires the best for each of its members, even those who differ violently or become prodigals. Come what may, one remains a member of the family.

Service. On many Brethren dining tables in the 1940's and 1950's, a visitor was apt to see a small wooden pedestalled cup, on which was printed a logo identified as

Brethren Service. The cup was an ever-present reminder to the family members, who frequently sat down at that table for physical nourishment, that there were other "brothers" and "sisters" in the world who fared less well. There were those whose table was bare and whose home was perhaps no more substantial than a cardboard box in an alleyway or a thin refugee tent in a strange and barren place. The cup was to be graced with daily contributions to be used for sharing with those less fortunate.

Service to their fellow humans is part of the Brethren consciousness, if not the very heart of their faith. Brethren have been a people who, as Bonhoeffer put it, "go about doing good," rather than specializing in theology or liturgy. With the exception of the love feast, which still occupies a unique place among contemporary Christian rites, Brethren have not been noted by their formal worship but by their *service* to the total human community. Historic examples include honest and dependable dealings, ministries to both Union and Confederate soldiers during the Civil War, Brethren Volunteer Service, the Heifer Project, refugee settlement, disaster relief, homes for the aging, and many manifestations of caring in local communities.

While Brethren may have been defensive and protective of their tradition at some points, the record shows that they were nonetheless conscious of their calling to "wash the feet" of the world. There is no dispute over the Christ-model of the suffering servant, who came "not to be served, but to serve" (Matt. 20:28). And there is likewise a full endorsement of the concept of a Savior for the whole world, the accomplishment of whose mission depends upon the help of his disciples in every age.

The Brethren thus reach out to serve all people without discriminating on the basis of religion, race, political persuasion, or social standing. In such service there is a definite sense of relationship with and responsibility to every man, woman, and child of the world. We are bound together with others under the God who created us all.

Reconciliation. It was reported to a pastor-parish relations committee of a local Brethren congregation that a small group of persons within the fellowship had voiced acute discontent over an aspect of the church's social ministry. The committee recognized within the group some perennial "rabble rousers" and toyed with the idea of passing it off and proceeding with business as usual. But the dismissal of the matter was not that easy. There was trouble in the family: The family's togetherness and united effectiveness was broken and threatened. The committee felt a compulsion to deal with that. Someone referred to Matthew 18. It was resolved that the committee would offer to sit down with the dissenters and attempt to restore harmony.

Although their history reports division, and the church itself was born out of schism, Brethren have never been comfortable with divisiveness, either within or without the church. One of the cardinal scriptures of Brethren consciousness is 2 Corinthians 5:16-21:

> From now on, therefore, we regard no one from a human point of view; even though we once regarded Christ from a human point of view, we regard him thus no longer. Therefore, if any one is in Christ, he is a new creation; the old has passed away, behold, the new has come. All this is from God, who through Christ reconciled us to himself and gave us the ministry of reconciliation; that is, in Christ God was reconciling the world to himself, not counting their trespasses against them, and entrusting to us the message of reconciliation. So we are ambassadors for Christ, God making his appeal through us. We beseech you on behalf of Christ, be reconciled to God. For our sake he made him to be sin who knew no sin, so that in him we might become the righteousness of God.

Brethren have taken seriously the calling to be "ambassadors of reconciliation." It is told that time and again in the early years of the World Council of Churches, the lone Brethren delegate, M. R. Zigler, was called upon within the General Assembly to settle disputes between other delegates voicing seemingly opposite viewpoints. As we have seen, Brethren have been on the forefront of restoring friendly relationships between America and countries behind the Iron Curtain. Brethren leadership has penetrated the ranks of the Fellowship of Reconciliation, and many local human relations councils. The Brethren have maintained a witness against racial prejudice and a program to encourage equal opportunity and respect. During the civil rights revolution of the 1960's the Brethren employed a national staff person to act as an impartial mediator in community conflicts. Many community leaders on both sides of the struggle hailed his effectiveness and expressed appreciation for the role played by the Brethren in that time of tension.

Floyd Mitchell states unequivocally, "Being Brethren calls us to work for the unity of the church" (*Brethren Life and Thought,* Vol. 20, Fall 1975, p. 228.). He would undoubtedly not object if we added to his proclamation the words, "and of the world." There is a Brethren consciousness which earnestly desires the angelic "peace and goodwill among men," and which accepts unequivocally a primary responsibility to work toward that end.

No privileged status. A visiting minister was escorted onto the stage of a Brethren fellowship hall to speak to a dinner gathering of expectant lay persons. The atmosphere was suddenly formal . . . heads turned slightly toward the stage, persons sat upright in their chairs, the uneasiness that accompanies a conscious attempt to do the correct thing. With a split-second analysis the minister retraced his journey upward until he stood, without podium or elevation, beside the front tables. "I would rather speak from here if it's okay," he announced. Chairs shuffled, sighs were released, *and ears were opened.*

Part of the Brethren consciousness is that distinctiveness in status, title, or privilege is not sanctioned in the

" . . . being Brethren calls us to work for the unity of the church."

new life of the kingdom. "In Christ there is neither Greek nor Jew, male nor female, slave or freeman (Gal. 3:28). Furthermore, all baptized believers are made ministers for Christ, called to a shared priesthood with him. The Brethren are uncomfortable with labels and with the valuation of one human group as better than another (especially as these distinctions apply to the church).

This rejection of special status for individuals points naturally to rejecting special status for any one church in the total body of Christ. Any claim to be superior to other parts of Christ's family runs contrary to our historic commitment to be on one level with each other. The biblical admonition not to think of ourselves more highly than we ought to think (Rom. 12:3) prevents us from standing proudly aloof from other Christians.

The characteristics we have described, what we have chosen to call the "Brethren consciousness," support the denomination's natural participation in reconciling the church to itself and to its Lord. Furthermore, the gifts of family concern, unreserved service, reconciling the broken, and rejecting special status, equip Brethren to contribute in very specific ways to any promising effort toward unifying the church.

Chapter 10

Beginning in Jerusalem — or Hickory Hollow

For purposes of this study it would be appropriate if we could emend Samuel Shoemaker's famous one sentence prayer, "Revive thy church, O Lord, beginning with me," so that it reads, "Restore unity to thy church, O Lord, beginning with our congregation!" All of us are in touch with a local church. It is within the local parish fellowship that we give tangible evidence of our belief in Jesus Christ. It is in frequent and regular contacts with other confessors that we have a context for sharing our convictions, hopes, fears, miseries, hatreds, and loves.

The local congregation is still the base of operations for the church of Jesus Christ. Just as the synagogue is the vehicle of memory, nurture, and growth for the world's dispersed Jews, who cannot make frequent journeys to the Jerusalem temple, so is the local congregation (and size is immaterial!) the rallying point for the Christian faith. It is there that the primary faith story is told and learned, practiced and proclaimed, right within the arena of real life.

The congregation is not the sum total of Christ's Church. Neither is it intended to be an entity within itself. The church into which each of us is baptized is much larger than the familiar group which frequently gathers at Hickory Hollow Church of the Brethren. We shall expand on this idea in succeeding sessions. But before we can successfully relate to the *whole body* of God's people, we must learn the rubrics of love and apply them to the primary testing ground of our discipleship, the local congregation.

The New Testament is a prolific source of models for congregational harmony and unity. 1 Corinthians 12—13, Ephesians 4, Colossians 3:12-17, and 1 Peter 3:8-17 are all primary passages. In this chapter we will explore the first of these texts in depth.

A quick overview of the Corinthian congregation unveils a situation uncomfortably common in our experience at Hickory Hollow. Uniting two ports on the trade route between east and west, Corinth had a very cosmopolitan culture. It was a breeding place for many religions and ideologies, among them the cult of the Greek goddess of love, Aphrodite. Corinthians characterized in Greek plays were always inebriated. The city had a world-wide reputation of containing every form of vice.

Paul implies in 1 Corinthians 6:9-10 that some of the persons now a part of the Corinthian church were formerly among the pleasure seekers of the Corinthian society. There is still disturbing evidence of its influence in the church: party spirit, disgracing the Lord's Supper, bickering and jealousy, slander and dishonesty, an unhealthy fighting for power within the church. Obviously out of much prayer and labor, Paul puts together in 1 Corinthians 12 and 13 a case for the essential unity of the church.

The apostle affirms at the outset that the unity of the church will be a unity in diversity. In 12:4-6 he makes clear that a common confession of faith does not imply uniformity of personality and ability. "There are varieties of gifts (within the church) even though it is the same Spirit, and there are varieties of working, even though it is the same God who inspires them all." Acceptance of our brothers and sisters in unity begins with the recognition that we do not all think alike, have like needs, nor are endowed with the same skills. Neither should we be critical or jealous of another's gifts, because all are given by God.

Paul was concerned about the tendency of the Corinthians to rate the worth of persons on the basis of the particular gift they exercised. The average congregation today sometimes falls into the same trap, measuring the value of persons by how well they perform certain functions deemed desirable. Persons who can play the piano, chair a commission, teach a church school class, give a "beautiful prayer," are often referred to as "wonderful churchmen" (or women).

Paul is seeking to puncture a hole in that way of thinking. There is intrinsic worth to every person quite apart from his or her endowed abilities. But even so, *every* person has some value in the functioning of the fellowship. Instead of assigning preference points to specific gifts, each person's gift should be honored and cherished for the good of the whole (see 12:7-11).

Paul proceeds then to strengthen his argument by introducing the metaphor of the body as a way of speaking about the church (12:12-26). Every one of his readers has an instant point of reference—his or her own body. What a motley combination of limbs, organs, veins, and functions! Yet each organ is a vital part of the whole body, and each is dependent upon the others. The people who constitute the church fellowship are to be regarded in the same way. Each member is a part of the body of Christ, the extension of Christ's physical presence today. Each member needs the other members of the body to keep the whole body functioning properly and adequately. Each is

" . . . each member needs the other members of the body to keep the whole functioning properly."

called to respect the functions of others, content to perform his or her own function, not coveting the others' tasks or honors. Each member is affected by the malfunction of the other, and as such is called upon to sympathize with and to help fulfill the ailing member's function.

The important emphasis in the idea of the body is the interrelatedness of the various members, even though there is a diversity in their functions and gifts: Equally important to our corporate identity is the fact that we are part of Jesus Christ himself, not just an institution. As we are intimately linked to one another, we are linked to Christ, and vice versa. "Inasmuch as you did it unto one of the least of these my brethren, you did it unto me" (Matt. 25:40).

There is no other Brethren experience which illustrates the corporateness of our life in Christ as profoundly and as inspirationally as the love feast. Not only do we celebrate the sacrifice of the body and blood of the Savior as redemption for our sin. We also demonstrate, on behalf of the serving Lord, our own "blood" relationship to our fellow brothers and sisters. We share with them a common meal (all are of equal worth) and set pride and place aside as we wash one another's feet. The love feast is more than a celebrative act of worship. It is also a service of healing and reconciliation, a service that restores the spirit of unity to the body.

Paul ends the discussion of the body with a promise to deliver an even more valuable way to effect unity in the church. Of course, we know he speaks of love (agape), the quality of life that he elsewhere claims can "knit every thing together" (Col. 3:14). 1 Corinthians 13:4-7 gives us a helpful list of those qualities of love that contribute toward unity and harmony within the congregation. (Keep in mind that 1 Corinthians 13 was written as a part of Paul's solution to end divisions and bickering within the church. Because the chapter has become a favorite reading for wedding services and in other ways been subjected to romanticizing, we have a tendency to forget its context. What a loss if we do not apply its truth to relationships within the church!)

The first of these qualities is *patience,* perhaps the very heart of love! Included in the virtue of patience are a whole host of self-disciplines: restraining temper, emotional control, listening, reasoning, objectivity, even empathy. Patience acknowledges that the other person with whom I am dealing, regardless of how offended I feel, has right to an opinion, and to the respect of being heard. Patience means that my opinion can even be withheld until others have a chance to give theirs.

Patience also means that I will try to "hear" another's point of view and not my preconception of that view. Jesus' purpose in Matthew 18:15-20 was to provide for this kind of depth reconciliation: "if he *listens* to you." And if one does *not* listen, then call in someone who can be impartial and objective, with both ears tuned in for truth and feelings.

The old admonition to "count to ten" before retaliating for an offense was not bad advice. It provided a moment for the heat of blind passion to subside and at least a partial vision of the opponent's worth to be regained.

Secondly, love is *kind.* Kindness in the Christian idiom is far more than courtesy. Kindness for the Christian is carrying a Roman soldier's heavy equipment two miles instead of the required one (Matt. 5:41); it is serving even the ingratiate (Luke 6:36). Kindness for the Christian means going beyond all that could possibly be expected of one in any situation. "You have done more than your share," we sometimes tell a hard worker. That extra effort is normative for the Christian who is working for unity with fellow Christians.

Thirdly, love *"does not insist on its own way."* A synonym for this desirable trait is "humility." The contrast between arrogance, or always wanting one's own way, and humility was evident in the story of Adam (Gen. 3:5). The primary sin of Adam was that he wanted to be like God. He wanted to be free from God, to be ruler of a world of his own in which everything happened just as he wanted it to happen, in which everything was subject to his will.

Such arrogance often is observed in the attitudes of church members, who expect everyone to think as they do. It is an attitude that readily contributes toward brokenness and division in the fellowship.

Finally, love *never ends*. It is a statement about the quality of love, but also an admonition about the quantity of love required of the Christian. "in *everything* put on love" (1 Cor. 16:14), "make love your aim" (1 Cor. 14:1), "speak the truth in love" (Eph. 4:15). All are phrases the apostle uses to encourage the unceasing use of love to govern every relationship. To reach a creative conclusion to any conflict between individuals there must be a commitment to love the other person no matter what the result. It is not necessary to agree with others in order to love them. Christian love does not always involve liking other persons or sanctioning their behavior. But it definitely demands of us that we seek the greatest possible good for the other.

Paul summarizes the spirit of unity that should exist within the congregation in his words to the Ephesians:

> I therefore, a prisoner for the Lord, beg of you to lead a life worthy of the calling to which you have been called, with all lowliness and meekness, with patience, forebearing one another in love, eager to maintain the unity of the Spirit in the bond of peace. There is one body and one Spirit, just as you were called to the one hope that belongs to your call, one Lord, one faith, one baptism, one God and Father of us all, who is above all and through all and in all.

> (Ephesians 4:1-6)

Chapter 11

Brethren Who Need
Other Brethren

Dr. James D. Glasse, President of Lancaster Theological Seminary, observed in a recent address that "the significant differences now are not between denominations but *within them*. We cannot hear the name of someone's denomination and know what he stands for. . . . Although there are still functional differences between denominations, the kind of things that used to divide denominations, are now what divide us within denomination. There's a kind of ecumenism *within* the denomination that now saps our energy" (a presentation to the 32nd Annual Assembly of the Council of Churches of Greater Harrisburg, January 16, 1976).

Dr. Glasse's thesis can be documented with recent religious news stories. The Southern Presbyterians and the Missouri Synod Lutherans have both experienced turmoil and division within their respective communions over doctrinal and biblical interpretation. The Episcopalians have had their internal waters troubled by a break with the tradition prohibiting the ordination of women to the priesthood. Though these three examples have received the most publicity, many other denominations are experiencing some degree of divisiveness or agitation.

The Church of the Brethren is no exception. This is documented in a superbly researched sociological case study of the denomination by Robert Blair and J. Henry Long ("Modernization and Subgroup Formation in a Religious Organization: A Case Study of the Church of the Brethren," *Brethren Life and Thought,* Vol. 22, 1976).

According to Blair and Long, there have been twenty-nine major cleavages within the church in its 270 year history. The most significant of these, in terms of numbers and impact upon the total Brethren presence, were the Ephrata separation in 1728, the Kentucky rebellion in 1826 (over the desired mode of feetwashing), and the Old Order and Progressive Brethren secessions in 1881 and 1882.

The most recent cleavages listed by Blair and Long consist of such subgroups as the Brethren Revival Fellowship (BRF), which is concerned with "the decline of biblical authority in the denomination"; the Brethren Peace Fellowship (BPF), rallying BVS alumni and others to preserve peace and heritage concerns for the church; and the Brethren charismatic movement, a loosely organized group which emphasizes renewal through the Holy Spirit and counts "baptism in the Spirit" as normative for full Christian experience. To these should be added another group called the Womaen's Caucus, concerned with the opportunities and interests of women within the church.

While citing the political influence of the subgroups within the denomination, Blair and Long do not believe that the conditions that could lead to schism by the groups are present. In particular, none of the sub-groups "have laid claim to a superior ideology which is interpreted as the only true expression of the Brethren tradition" (*Ibid.*, p. 229). Furthermore, the groups all seem to have as an objective to seek change *within* the church, rather than separate themselves from the larger body.

Clearly, however, there is fragmentation within the denomination. Even though there may not be a propensity for schism, conflict is inevitable as the groups put pressure for recognition of their causes on the denominational leadership and membership at large, as well as on each other.

The challenge is to use this conflict constructively. Note that the suggestion is not that the conflict among groups be eliminated, nor the groups themselves. The consensus among Brethren sociologists and historians seems to be that the presence of these specific emphases has a healthy kind of stabilizing effect upon the total life of the denomination. Furthermore, it is consistent with Brethren practice to "let everyone speak" and to weigh each opinion with careful and courteous consideration.

Before proceeding further, it may be well to try to identify some typically Brethren ways of dealing with diversity and opposing viewpoints. These observations from our heritage can provide clues on how to promote unity in the midst of conflict today.

1. In spite of the schisms and cleavages which have occurred in its history, the Church of the Brethren has always had a bias toward maintaining unity. In earlier decisions of the church this was carried to extreme, so that *no* decision was ever made until there was *unanimous* consent. The 1815 Annual Meeting instructed its delegates: "The Lord Jesus and the apostles teach us that we should be one, of one mind, speak the same thing, and that there should be no division among us." Numerous votes were often taken on matters of polity and belief before unanimity was reached! The principle at work here was that of keeping the denominational family together and united in

their witness. It was not unanimity for unanimity's sake, but the genuine desire to be one in Christ and in obedience to his will.

The rule of unanimity is, of course, no longer used in the councils and conferences of the church. Its impracticality impaired the urgency of carrying the gospel mission to the world. But the basic principle still affects denominational and congregational decision. Often in Annual Conference a moderator will rule on the final vote of a controversial issue by adding a plea that "we support the decision of the majority in the spirit of Brethren unity." Blair and Long note that denominational leaders are increasingly willing to accomodate their own interests of those capable of challenging their authority. The church publications, *Messenger* and *Brethren Life and Thought,* provide space for the airing of all viewpoints within the church and encourage articles which attempt to synthesize and bring these viewpoints together. Though unanimity is no longer a realistic goal, we still strive for a consensus that catches up everyone's concerns.

2. Brethren have a strong Judeo-Christian sense of corporate belonging, in which no one is dispensable. Each individual and/or each group within the church is seen as an essential part of the whole, which cannot be separated or severed without significant injury or handicap to the whole. The principle is the body/parts analogy of 1 Corinthians 12.

In the close-knit community every person and every group of persons take on real and recognized personalities. One marvels at how familiar an Annual Conference moderator is with the majority of those who come to the microphones to speak on issues, calling most of them by first names. Likewise, sub-groups are not just impersonal political entities within the church. They are known by the personalities and sincerity of their individual members, all of whom are important to the denominational family in many other ways, totally apart from their sub-group interests (e. g. as relatives, pastors, fellow college alumni, writers evangelists, ad infinitum). They stand as "brothers" and "sisters" to all others—quite apart from any ideological differences with others for which they may at times, or consistently, crusade.

3. It follows then that, for Brethren, people (persons) are more important than ideologies. When sickness, death, tragedies, disaster, and the like occur, the "labels" are disregarded and the true "brotherhood" is evoked. One substantiating example is that of a congregation in which a certain man sought to block nearly every progressive idea advanced for the worship and ministry of the church. He seemed alone in his consistent resistance to change, much to the consternation of pastor and congregation. Yet, when the irate member's barn caught fire one Sunday morning, the church services were suspended so that other members could assist with the fire-fighting and the protection of the adjoining buildings!

4. Brethren believe that the Holy Spirit is revealed in various ways and that no two persons necessarily receive or manifest the Spirit and the Spirit's gifts in the same manner. To one, God may give the quiet manner of scholarship and deliberateness, to another a hightly emotionally charged, impulsive enthusiasm. By one the Spirit may be most deeply felt in quiet meditation; by another in a pentecostal experience. For this reason the Brethren are reluctant to be judgmental of the religious experience of groups or individuals. Freedom of individual conscience and religious interpretation are respected within the church.

So much for insights from our heritage. Given the fragmentation which continues to be a reality in the church, how can we build up the body? What guidelines can help promote unity between Brethren rather than allowing the cleavages to grow wider?

1. All groups must find their starting point, their raison d'etre, in Jesus Christ. It is *his* body we are to build. Each group should ask: "Are our objectives in keeping with his teaching and example? Are we fulfilling a need of the body, or simply being carried as an extra wheel or parasitic baggage?" Not only does Christ provide a point of origin at which all groups are one. He also is the ultimate evaluation of a group's authenticity and worth.

2. It must be recognized that the religious perspective of every person is shaped by his or her background, experiences, and a particular set of relationships with God and other persons. Paul was combating in Corinth the tendency of one group to lord it over all the others, to claim they had the only and best way. All who are satisfied with their religious experience should have that experience confirmed and honored by all others whose experience may differ. No group should be overbearing or judgmental in its attitude toward the other groups.

3. It must be remembered that the power of the Holy Spirit cannot be limited nor defined by human ability. It is the Holy Spirit who makes possible the unity and the ongoing work of the church, and the Holy Spirit comes as the enabler in many ways: "Now there are varieties of gifts, but the same Spirit; and there are varieties of service, but the same Lord; and there are varieties of working, but it is the same God who inspires them all in every one. To each is given the manifestation of the Spirit for the common good" (1 Cor. 12:4-7). As Alan Walker observes in his book *Breakthrough*: "Paul does not relate the baptism of the Spirit only to some special act of service and witness. He does not confine the Spirit merely to charismatic moments or for notable preaching or spectacular revivalism. Paul sees the Spirit as the power behind all of us, wherever we serve, whatever we do within the normal, regular strategy of the Church of Jesus Christ" (p. 49).

" . . . all are called to remain open to . . . learn from others."

4. All groups must strive for *truth* in communicating their concerns. Research and clarity are cardinal virtues and attention should be given to matters that are significant. Frequently divisions are prompted by misunderstandings or misrepresentations of others' viewpoints. It is possible also for surface issues, like language or methodology, to precipitate a rift that really has no substance. (Remember the famous Paris Talks where the shape of the table was hotly debated before the talks could proceed?)

5. All must make a sincere effort to hear and understand one another's point of view. Concerns should be addressed generally to the whole body and not promote mutiny or ingrownness. Literature should stress those things which are constructive for the whole and not supportive of division or further fragmentation.

6. All groups must frequently affirm and work together on mutual concerns, not hesitating to cross lines to identify with a cause another group is championing.

7. Each group should recognize the right of others to differ. Even in the face of serious disagreements, groups should not demand the capitulation of one side to another.

8. All are called to remain open to new truth and insights, especially as each can learn from the other. God's revelation is not closed. Dialogue should be kept going between each other, as well as with God. The way should always be left open for concilation.

Chapter 12

Relating to Other Clans

Paul was not only interested in maintaining unity among local fellowship groups like those at Corinth. He also sought to build a closer kinship among all of the new Christian communities: He shared with them the news of what other congregations were doing (e.g. 2 Cor. 8:1-2). He reported what others thought of them (1 Th. 1:6-7). He took any promising "missionaries" from local congregations with him on his journeys (Col. 4:12). He urged communication and fellowship among those churches in the same geographic vicinity (Col. 4:15). There seems also to be evidence that the apostle paved the way for the transfer of membership from one community's congregation to another. Further, we are aware that Paul conducted an offering for the church at Jerusalem among the predominately Gentile churches of Asia. He did this as a means of promoting a bond of unity, as well as to bail out the financially troubled "mother church."

The point of this session is that, just as Brethren need

other Brethren, so do Christians need other Christians. No congregation can exist in a vacuum. It will soon become ingrown and will eventually die from lack of the stimuli of growth and challenge. Neither can a denomination survive in isolation from other parts of the body. An organ whose veins are severed from relationship to other organs soon withers and dies. It has no further use nor stimulus apart from the rest of the body. Isolationism and independence, whether congregational or denominational, fails to recognize the social inter-relatedness of the race. It also overlooks the magnitude of the redemptive task that must be done if the kingdom is to come on earth. Consider the following vignettes of actual communities, as reported in *Ecumenical Designs,* an action / study booklet provided by the Steering Committee of the National Consultation on the Church in Community Life, 1967:

The big red fire truck came roaring down the street with siren blaring, red light flashing and a host of automobiles following in its wake. With their newly purchased equipment the volunteer fire company of a small village was on its way to the scene of a chimney fire at a farm house nearby. The men of the village and surrounding area have worked diligently to make their fire company and equipment second to none. They are proud of their achievements and their spirits are high because of the fruits of their common endeavor. These men represent a cross section of the community and no special social qualifications are required of them for participation. They belong! The president of the organization is a clerk in the village general store. The chief of the company is a laborer in a nearby shoe factory. The treasurer is the cashier of the local bank. Members include the local insurance agent, clerk in the post office, gas station attendant, the millwright, and a host of men who are drawn together by their common concern for the safety of their homes and the civic well-being of their community. The company serves as a civic organization. It provides the stimulus for community events such as: village Christmas trees, Halloween parade, Soapbox Derby and Christmas baskets for the needy.

Though these men can labor together in the fire company, Sunday morning finds them sitting apart in four churches of small membership. Two churches are located in the village while

" . . . as Brethren need other Brethren, so do Christians need
other Christians."

the others are located in the rural area immediately adjacent. Some of the men travel to the Church of the Brethren, a mile and a half east of the village, where the only resident pastor serves a congregation of 200 members. Others go north to the Evangelical United Brethren Church where there's a strong Sunday School, but where worship services are held only every other week. Still others are to be found in the two small churches in the village—a Lutheran and a Methodist—each served by a pastor who lives elsewhere and visits these churches as part of a circuit parish. As church members they know each other well, but it has never occurred to them that they could worship together. Somehow being a Brethren, a Lutheran, a Methodist, or an E.U.B. marks them as individuals—separate but equal. The reasons for separation have passed with the passing of the generations. They have grown accustomed to limited service and leadership on the part of their pastors and are satisfied with the attention they receive. They do not expect much from their church and have become victims of their low desire.

In many respects the fire company is more relevant to the people than is the church. No matter how imperfect it may be, the fire company brings the men together in a meaningful way and provides a channel through which their civic and benevolent impulses may be positively expressed. It is—for all practical purposes—a substitute religion. The church is hopelessly fragmented and offers little to meet the real needs of the people—only a continuing struggle to survive as separate denominational entities.

****

"Business as usual," "tending the sheep within the fold," "sticking to spiritual matters as we ought" are frequently used cliches. They salve our collective consciences in the church and prevent significant involvement in the secular society in which the church exists.

In a large town (some may call it a small city) of 22,000 population, six large Protestant churches and one Roman Catholic Church were busy enlarging their facilities for parochial schools and expanding programs. Competition for new members continued apace; financial compaigns to underwrite budgets and buildings were waged successfully; the official bodies of all the churches met regularly to consider pressing problems such as janitorial services, choir music, payment of bills, etc.; and each church was marked by commonly accepted standards of success with fine buildings, big budgets successfully underwritten, and continued membership participation.

Meanwhile, three attempts to pass a school bond issue failed without any real support or opposition from the churches or their pastors. Instead, it was the combined efforts of the community service clubs that finally passed the needed bond issue. But who or what agency shall deal with the pressing problems of that town: alcoholism, high school dropouts, unwed mothers, high divorce rate, the development of a community college, ministry to inmates of a nearby penal institution, and the racial ghetto within its bounds? And what of the world problems which must be confronted—hunger, disease, poverty, war, population explosion, etc.? Shall these too be referred to the service club or some other agency while the church continues "to stick to spiritual matters?"

No Council of Churches existed through which the church people could discuss community and world issues and channel their energies in the direction of solutions. The ministerial association served primarily as a means for the members to keep an eye on one another. "Successful" churches adhered to "the spiritual matters," affirming their impotency for any constructive involvement in the community.

In the first example there is the implication that the denominational churches, existing completely independent of one another, were not touching base with the reality of the daily life of the townspeople. Instead of speaking to relationships, the Sunday morning hour was the one time the town was severely divided! The people had to create another vehicle to discover and celebrate community!

The second example reveals that in this typical community the collective church *could* be the greatest single force for change and improvement. But because each congregation was intent upon advancing its own program, the influence of the church in the community was practically nil.

The metaphor of the body in 1 Corinthians 12 is just as relevant for the ecumenical church as it is for the individual congregation. The body includes *all* of Christ's believers and followers, and the parts of the body include denominations and communions, as well as individual members. How the body functions is determined by the way the gifts of the members are deployed. It is not *what gift* each part can *bring* to the body, but *what gifts the body needs* that each individual part can supply. This important distinction is also a clue to how the body can function properly and effectively. The body needs a heart, so one individual organ can supply a pumping action. The body needs sight, so one individual organ develops the capacity to see, and so forth. The functions of the parts are conditioned and created by the needs of the body. It is the body which determines the role of the parts and not vice versa!

This is not to say that the body becomes a glorified smelting pot in which the parts lose their identity and are molded into mute ingots. On the contrary, the importance of each part is borne out in the fact that it is performing a function for the body that no other part is doing. Yet each part is contributing (equally and significantly) toward the whole.

Such collegiality can happen in Christianity if denominational groups can develop a sense of dependence upon and accountability to one another.

Accountability is an important term for our consideration. To be accountable, according to the Random House Dictionary means "subject to report, explain, justify, answer to." Accountability thus implies a relationship deeper than co-existence or even cooperation. It suggests a responsibility to one another for behavior and being.

How can accountability occur? Here are several observations:

1. *Accountability among churches of different faith backgrounds is dependent upon the willingness and commitment of those churches (and especially their leadership) to be in dialogue with others and to interact with them.*

Exhibit: The United Methodist Church of Shanesburg developed a proposal for involving the town's five churches in a joint study-education seminar related to the future of the area of Shanesburg. The situation leading to the proposal was that so many of the young people, following college, were moving to larger metropolitan areas. The United Methodist Church's administrative council felt it was a matter which merited joint consultation and formally invited the other churches to respond. Three of the remaining communions forwarded enthusiastic responses, along with commitments to send representatives to an agreed-upon meeting. The fourth church did not reply, and when contacted by phone, the pastor was non-committal, stating that the people thought it was a good idea but they probably could not get anyone to participate in the study. They would send someone if they could.

The seminar took the form of a series of several sessions, about half of which were attended by the pastor of the non-committal church. Some strategies were proposed on an evening when there was no representative from the fifth church. There was some reservation expressed about moving ahead with four-fifths of the Christian community, but the consensus was that the project could not wait.

2. *Accountability resides in the desire to be of use by contributing denominational uniqueness and strength toward a common goal, rather than by imposing sectarian bias.*

Exhibit: The Skyridge Church of the Brethren, Kalamazoo, Michigan, a congregation with only twenty-one families, observed that two of its closest neighboring congregations were engaged in a similar struggle to provide full-time services and fellowship activities for their constituency. The other two congregations were the Kalamazoo Mennonite Congregation and the Judson Baptist Church. The Brethren, utilizing their style of openness and conciliation, took the initiative in suggesting that the three congregations hold union

111

summer worship services. People would meet in each of the three churches for four consecutive weeks, the respective pastors having responsibilities for four services each and arranging their summer schedules according to vacation and conference events.

This venture led to the formation of an Interchurch Relations Committee among the three congregations, which utilized the strengths of each communion to provide joint study, worship, and fellowship opportunities throughout the entire year. Brethren pastor John Tomlonson summarized the results of the joint effort by saying "Feelings of 'we-ness' have begun to replace feelings of 'them' and 'us.'" (Though this venture is not currently operative, the model remains a valid one.)

3. *Accountability among two or more congregations or judicatories means responsibility to offer community services that do not duplicate or cancel out what others are already effectively doing.*

Exhibit: The Roman Catholic parish in the uptown section of a medium-sized city had maintained an effective drug information and rehabilitation center for three years. It had consistently invited participation and input from all sectors of the community and had likewise offered the services of the center to all. The ministry was funded by the area diocese, as well as through an estate endowment, and was thus well-staffed and alert to the latest techniques and data.

One of the nearby Protestant churches became alarmed when the police referred a young person from that congregation to the Catholic center for thereapy. Fearful that this might lead to "a domination of Catholic belief in our city," the board of the Protestant church hastily acted to hire a full-time youth-worker. His task would be "to warn the youth of our church and community of the dangers of taking drugs and to advise them regarding the true teachings of Jesus Christ and His

Church." In this instance, distrust prevented a spirit of accountability and led to a competitive ministry.

4. *Accountability is achieved in direct proportion to the degree of trust established between clans.*

Exhibit: Faith Presbyterian Church and Highview Church of the Brethren maintained separate facilities and ministries less than two blocks away from each other. Both were aware that their respective church school were dwindling in attendance, mainly because quality teachers were difficult to recruit. While sharing about their common problem over a cup of coffee in the local diner one morning, the pastors of the two churches wondered if some sort of combined church school, using the best teachers from each congregation, might be possible. As they discussed the idea in their commissions on education, a plan of implementation began to form., which sought to build in an undergirding level of trust.

First, both pastors issued statements affirming commitment to the idea and suggesting there was no intent to proselytize members from one communion to the other. A similar statement from each of the administrative boards went into the plan, along with a commitment to arrange for both congregations a seminar on the history and beliefs of each denomination. When joint church school classes began, they were held at both locations, with the age groups having the largest Brethren makeup meeting in the Presbyterian Church and vice versa. Curriculum was chosen by a joint task committee, in consultation with the teachers.

The mission of Jesus Christ could be greatly enhanced and advanced if there were more dialogue, sharing and combining of resources among the faith communities within Christendom. Although many experimental programs and federations are operating with notable success, cooperation and interaction has barely begun. The possibilities for local cluster activities and sharing across

113

denominational lines are unlimited, without the loss of identity by any.

Chapter 13

To Reconcile All Things

The church is not an institution to be "enjoyed as one would patronize a play or a professional ball game. The church is ordained by God for a vital purpose: to facilitate the coming of the kingdom of God and to unite *all of the human family* in the kingdom's fellowship.

Much has been said throughout this study about the unity of the church, based upon the belief that Christ is the body, that Christians and denominations are functioning parts of that Body. The unity of the church depends upon each part functioning in relation to, though distinct from the others.

But we dare not stop there, for we would have created a mere machine that has no purpose. John 3:16-17 gives us the clue to the body's purpose: "For God so loved the world that he gave his only Son, that whoever believes in him should not perish but have eternal life. For God sent the Son into the world, not to condemn the world, but that the world might be saved through him." So likewise when Jesus prays that the disciples may become one in John 17, he prays not "for these only, but also for those who believe in me through their word, that they may *all* be one" (17:20). The whole world is to be united and reconciled to the Creator, God.

Paul points to the same hope in his letter to the Romans: "For the creation waits with eager longing for the revealing of the sons of God; for the creation was subjected to futility, not of its own will but by the will of him who subjected it in hope; because the creation itself will be set free from its bondage to decay and obtain the glorious liberty of the children of God" (Rom. 8:19-21). Similarly, the author of 2 Peter asserts: "According to his promise we wait for new heavens and a new earth on which righteousness dwells" (2 Pet. 3:13, cf. Rev. 21:1-5).

The quest for unity does not stop with the unity of Christians in the church, but anticipates the unity of all humankind, the solidarity of the whole world family. Augustin Cardinal Bea has said: "No Christian is a true Christian unless he feels his responsibility for the whole of the human family and is moved by sincere love for it. It is *his* family and all men are his brothers. . . . The Christian knows that Christ is not only the 'Prince of Peace' (Isaiah 9:6) but he is 'our peace' (Ephesians 2:14), the peace of the whole of mankind, for he is its Savior and its peace through time and eternity" (*Unity in Freedom,* p. 231).

The church is the colony of heaven on earth, the visible demonstration of the quality of life and promise of hope exemplified by the crucified and resurrected Lord of Lords. The resources of the colony promoting human unity and making an ideological impact on all phases and institutions of human life are unlimited. The church, by the grace and authority of God, in the name of the Risen Christ, and by the power of the Holy Spirit, *can* effect peace, goodwill, and the ultimate unity of all humanity.

Archimandrite Cyrille Argenti, dean of the Greek

" ... the quest for unity ... anticipates the unity of all humankind, the solidarity of the whole world family."

Orthodox parish in Marseilles, France, addressed a plenary session at the World Council of Churches Fifth Assembly in Nairobi with these words: "The unity of the church prepares the way for the unity of the world . . . This united community must, however, also behave in a way which shows that it really is the Body of Christ. This means that in its witness for justice, truth, and liberty it will not be afraid to lay itself open to persecution by the political power and the powerful of this world, for, as Paul tells us in his letter to Timothy: 'Persecution will come to all who want to live a godly life as Christians' (2 Tim. 3:12).

"It also means that through the love it shows to its enemies and its constant prayers for those who persecute it, it is a living witness to the Lamb who was sacrificed and rose again interceding for the world and saying through our mouths: 'Father, forgive them: they do not know what they are doing' (Luke 23:34).

"The church is therefore a witnessing community because it identifies itself with the Body of the Crucified and Risen Christ: this is the church in which we confess our faith in the words of the Creed: 'I believe in the One, Holy Catholic, and Apostolic Church'" (*The Ecumenical Review,* World Council of Churches, Vol 28, No. 1, January 1976, p. 31).

Argenti also said: "If we are not united, we are not the church; if we are not the church we are not the Body of Christ; and if we are not the Body of Christ, how is the world to know that He has risen and lives today" (*Ibid.* p. 30)?

The Nairobi Assembly went on the affirm that being the body of Christ also includes being about the ministry of Christ, leaving his marks among suffering humankind. "Christian witness has to do with Christians struggling against the power of evil within themselves, within the churches, and in society" (Report of the World Council, section on "Confessing Christ Today"). The whole church is called on to preach the whole gospel to the whole person and to the whole world. Clearly the church's sights should be set on no less farreaching goal than the realization of a global family.

The Nairobi Assembly listed in rather concise terms the agenda for the church's global concern:

1. Concern for the poor in their struggle against poverty and injustice.

2. Development of a sacramental view of nature toward the stewardship and renewal of the earth's resources.

3. Recovering and reaffirming the sanctity of all human life.

4. A call to nonviolence and disarmament throughout the world.

5. Continued concern regarding, and action to eliminate, world hunger.

6. Priority attention to the status and equality of women in church and society.

7. The right of every person to personal dignity and religious freedom.

8. Continued efforts to combat racism in economic, social and religious structures.

This is the agenda Christians need to address themselves to if they are to prepare the way to world unity.

In order for the church, be it the local congregation or the church universal, to effectively attend to its mandate, it must commit itself to a ministry of dialogue and confrontation with every existing organization for human change and order. The individualistic approach which seeks to convert persons one by one in the hope that the community will be redeemed is not enough. The church must speak to the *structures* of society as well.

On the local level, the church must carry its message

and extend its accountability to industries, corporations, judicial and governmental authorities, professional organizations, labor unions, and other secular institutions.

On the broader scale, the church must be concerned with efforts such as the United Nations, SALT negotiations, regional security pacts such as NATO, and other international vehicles for peace and order, human rights, environmental protection, and the like. And the church must continue its support of relief and rehabilitation efforts, such as Church World Service, Christian Overseas Relief, the Heifer Project, etc.

Finally, the church, to be the church, and the catalyst for unity among humankind, must learn to forget itself, as did the Savior, and risk the vulnerability of its life. Even Christianity itself is not as important as having all brothers and sisters "Dwell in unity!" (See Psalm 133.) Jesus said to the disciples "If any man would come after me let him deny himself and take up his cross and follow me" (Matt. 16:24). When that surrender is made, then the church, and subsequently the whole human family, will be in union with the creator and with each other.

Dr. J. Robert Nelson, one of this century's greatest ecumenists, says: "In New Testament Greek there is an interesting word for 'time.' It is *kairos*. It means the 'right time' or the 'fulfilled time,' such as the time for harvesting grapes when they are neither too green nor too ripe, or the time for a woman to be delivered of her baby, or—especially for faith in Jesus Christ—the time for God to send his only Son into the world. Now it seems that in the history of church unions there is always a *kairos* to be watched for, a time that is just right for the talking to stop and the action to begin." (*Crisis in Unity and Witness,* p. 109).

APPENDICES

BIBLIOGRAPHY

STUDY SUGGESTIONS

Appendix 1

Audio-visual Resources

The following filmstrips relating to subject matter in this study are all available from:

Church of the Brethren District Filmstrip Library

Hiram J. Frysinger

5505 Union Deposit Road

Harrisburg, Pa. 17111

It is recommended that you order 3-4 weeks in advance of desired showing date. FS means filmstrip with script only, no record accompanying. SFS means "sound filmstrip," which includes a record (or in some cases also a cassette). Please order by number and title.

382 FS UNITED IN CHRIST. Explains the structure and work of the National Council of Churches.

382A SFS FIRST PERSON PLURAL. Describes purpose and action of the National Council, including scenes of service and ministry.

382F SFS WHERE THE WIND BLOWS. Interprets work of both World Council of Churches and the National Council of Churches. Illustrates the variety of ministries.

382N SFS THE COUNCIL OF NICAEA. Describes the persecution of Christians under Diocletion and the change to acceptance under Constantine. Depicts the Council's gathering to settle the doctrinal issue that threatened to divide the church.

388B-1 FS ASSIGNMENT IN UNITY (World Council of Churches). The World Council's purpose and work, with pictures from some of the earlier assemblies.

388B-2 FS ECUMENICAL—ARE WE? The term "ecumenicity" is visualized as the WCC work is viewed around the globe.

388C. FS THE WORLD IN A WORD. Presents meaning and importance of word "ecumenical." A historical treatment of the use of the word, and ziblical support for the ecumenical movement.

388D FS THE ECUMENICAL MOVEMENT. Interprets

meaning of word "ecumenical" and show how Christians have learned to work together. Encourages ecumenicity on the local scene.

388E SFS THE FOUNDATION FOR DIALOGUE. Opens with statement that there can be no dialogue without knowledge. Includes basic beliefs of the major communions and a message on loving each other from Pope Paul VI.

388F SFS A NEW PILGRIMAGE. Gives background information on COCU.

388H SFS THIS IS MY HERITAGE (American Baptist). Life and history of the Baptists.

414A SFS FOR GOD AND NEIGHBOR. A description of Brethren Volunteer Service.

414AB SFS THESE ARE MY PEOPLE. The story of Brethren Volunteer Service at home and abroad.

414 SFS UNTO THESE MY BRETHREN. Shows the basis, aims and work of Brethren Service in Europe.

414CH. SFS THE GIFT THAT MULTIPLIES. Describes work of the Heifer Project begun by Dan West in 1944.

414L-3 SFS THE HUNGRY FUTURE. Shows stark facts of world hunger and what the church can do about it. Very comprehensive treatment of the factors contributing to the current problem.

413 SFS MY PEACE I GIVE TO YOU. The worldwide program of the Church of the Brethren.

Statement by J. W. Lear
to the Council of Boards of the Church of the Brethren, 1928

The order given by Christ to his church is much too large for our small denomination to undertake alone. We may have just cause to maintain a separate denominational organization and overhead, but we certainly would not take to ourselves the credit of being Christ's only representative body. The institutionalism, ecclesiasticism, formalism, ritualism, sacerdotalism, etc., of the Roman Catholic Church created a mighty upheaval in the religious world in the fourteenth century, and in the protest which followed many denominations were formed. In the emphasis upon differences of interpretation of church policy, of church sacraments, etc., the agreements were often-times over-looked. A spirit of contention, competition, and hatred was engendered which closed the bowels of compassion and often turned the denominations into proselyting camps instead of soul-saving and soul-building institutions.

We have now come upon a new era. The day of religious debate has all but gone. Denominations are agreeing on a system of comity. A disposition to discover fundamental agreements is creating a spirit of togetherness. Denominations, having discovered that many of their tasks are common, are federating in religious work. Church union is in the air and is being picked up by the radio. The most popular magazines today are devoting a page or more to religious subjects, and not infrequently a note favorable to church union goes forth. The Federal Council of Churches was organized to foster agreement in spirit and federation in service. It is generally believed that Protestantism cannot long endure divided into one hundred and fifty camps. Conferences of several communions have appointed committees to study church union and devise methods of merging. The churches of Canada launched a formidable movement in that direction. The Congregational and New Light (Christian) fraternities are proposing and fostering a merger. The Reformed, the

Evangelical Synod, and the United Brethren denominations have committees collaborating with this end in view.

We will be expected to face the changing conditions along with other fraternities. Whether we stand still or go forward, we will be compelled by the inertia of the movement to speak out. Even our own people and especially the youth will sooner or later call for a pronouncement. We will be asked to justify the ground for our attitude of aloofness. We may have sufficient cause, I am not saying we have not. I am saying, however, that we will be expected and even forced to clarify and justify our position to our own people first of all, if we hope to hold their loyalty and challenge whole-hearted service, and also other Christian people must know that we have, at least, the semblance of worthiness if we are to hold their respect. And at last, but not least, we must be sure that the position which calls for independent relation and action is acceptable to him who said, "Neither for these do I pray, but for them also that believe on me through their word; that they may all be one; even as thou, Father, are in me and I in thee, that they may be one is us; that the world may believe that thou didst send me."

There is no reason in becoming panicky, as some seem inclined. To throw up our hands and say we are doomed to be crushed in the movement is foolish. Let us be sane and clear-headed. Let no one think of abandoning our position till we are sure of our ground. We are not justified in junking the ship until we are assured of a better one. We have no excuse for losing our loyalties to the old denomination until we are sure that the new loyalties are more Christlike. If the time for a merger should come in our day, those who are most loyal to the denomination could contribute most wisely in the new alignment. Moreover, these statements are not projected to inspire sentiment toward church union, but rather to provoke an honest, intelligent search for the position we should take under God in a day like this.

Appendix 3

A Litany for
the Various Communions

Let us give thanks for the gifts and graces of each major division of Christendom:

For the ROMAN CATHOLIC CHURCH, its glorious traditions, its disciplines in holiness, its worship, rich with the religious passion of the centuries; its noble company of martyrs, doctors, and saints;

We thank thee, O Lord, and bless thy holy name.

For the EASTERN ORTHODOX CHURCH, its secret treasure of mystic experience; its marvelous liturgy; its regard for the collective life and its common will as a source of authority;

We thank thee, O Lord, and bless thy holy name.

For the great Protestant and evangelical communions:

For the CONGREGATIONALIST concern for the rightful independence of the soul and of the group;

We thank thee, O Lord, and bless thy holy name.

For the BAPTIST churches, stressing personal regeneration and the conscious relation of the mature soul to its Lord;

We thank thee, O Lord, and bless thy holy name.

For power among METHODISTS to awaken the conscience of Christians to our social evils; and for their emphasis upon the witness of experience and the fruits of the disciplined life;

We thank thee, O Lord, and bless thy holy name.

For the PRESBYTERIAN reverence for the sovereignty of God and their confidence in his faithfulness to his covenant; for their sense of the moral law, expressing itself in constitutional government;

We thank thee, O Lord, and bless thy holy name.

For the witness to the perpetual real presence of the inner light in every human soul borne by the RELIGIOUS SOCIETY OF FRIENDS and for their faithful continuance of a free prophetic ministry and Christian non-violence;

We thank thee, O Lord, and bless thy holy name.

For the LUTHERAN CHURCH, its devotion to the grace of

God and the Word of God, enshrined in the ministry of the Word and sacraments;

We thank thee, O Lord, and bless thy holy name.

For the ANGLICAN CHURCH; its reverent and temperate ways, through its Catholic heritage and its Protestant conscience; its yearning over the divisions of Christendom, and its longing to be used as a house of reconciliation;

We thank thee, O Lord, and bless thy holy name.

For the numberless FREE CHURCHES, many humble and without comeliness, in slum and country place and town, speaking the gospel to those unwelcome or uninspired in other congregations;

We thank thee, O Lord, and bless thy holy name.

O God, grant unto all these families within thy great Church, that as they come from the East and from the West to sit down in thy kingdom, each may lay at thy feet that special grace and excellence with which thou in times past hast endowed it, in Christ. Amen.

(From the Federal Council Bulletin, 1940, abridged in *The Student Prayerbook*, Haddam House, 1953, pp. 137-138)

SELECTED BIBLIOGRAPHY

Augustin Cardinal Bea, *Unity in Freedom.* New York: Harper and Row, 1964.

Richard A. Bollinger, *The Church in a Changing World.* Elgin: The Brethren Press, 1965.

Brethren Life and Thought, Volumes 11, 12, 21.

Donald F. Durnbaugh, ed., *The Church of the Brethren Past and Present.* Elgin: The Brethren Press, 1971.

Donald F. Durnbaugh, *European Origins of the Brethren.* Elgin: The Brethren Press, 1958.

Ecumenical Designs. New York: Committee on Studies, National Consultation on the Church in Community Life, 1967.

The Ecumenical Review, Volume 28.

Harold E. Fey, ed., *The Ecumenical Advance. A History of the Ecumenical Movement,* Volume 2, 1948-1968. Philadelphia: Westminster Press, 1970.

Charles W. Forman, *A Faith for the Nations.* Philadelphia: Westminster Press, 1957.

George L. Hunt and Paul A. Crow, Jr., eds., *Where We Are In Church Union.* New York: Association Press, 1965.

Minutes of the Church of the Brethren Annual Conferences, 1956-1976.

Lesslie Newbigin, *The Household of God.* New York: Friendship Press, 1954.

Listen Pope, *The Kingdom Without Caste.* New York: Friendship Press, 1957.

Ruth Rouse and Stephen C. Neill, eds., *A History of the Ecumenical Movement,* Volume 1, 1517-1948. Philadelphia: Westminster Press, 1954.

Roger Sappington, *The Brethren in the New Nation.* Elgin: The Brethren Press, 1976.

John R. Scotford, *Church Union—Why Not?* Boston: Pilgrim Press, 1948.

Barry Till, *The Churches' Search for Unity.* Baltimore: Penguin Books, 1972.

Maurice Villain, *Unity, a History and Some Reflections.* Baltimore: Helicon Press, 1963.

Willem Visser 't Hooft, *Has the Ecumenical Movement a Future?*
Atlanta: John Knox Press, 1976.

Williston Walker, *A History of the Christian Church,* 3rd ed.
New York: Scribners, 1970.

Lorell Weiss, *Therefore Brethren.* Elgin: The Brethren Press, n.d.

Colin W. Williams, *For the World.* New York: 1965.

World Council of Churches. Geneva/New York:

The Evanston Report, 1954

The New Delhi Report, 1962

The Uppsala Report, 1968

The Nairobi Report, 1976

Uppsala to Nairobi, Report of the Central Committee to the
Fifth Assembly of the World Council

SUGGESTED ACTIVITIES FOR GROUP STUDY

Chapter 1

1. Assign the characters of the dialogue to members of your class, then read the material as though you were Mr. Brown's class. Try to put feeling into your "play acting."

2. List on newsprint or a chalkboard the different positions which Mr. Brown's class members represent. Invite persons to indicate the positions that come closest to their own—and the reasons why. Explore further why we have different feelings about the question of church unity.

3. Divide into diads (two persons in each group) and share with each other your personal spiritual history: your denominational background, the personal significance of your baptism, your memories of religion at home when you were a child, special services, Annual Conference memories, pastors who have left impressions on your life, the church affiliations of your closest relatives, etc. Spend about twenty minutes in the diads, then reassemble as a class and have each person "introduce" the other person in his or her diad. Note ways in which you yourselves are an "ecumenical" group.

4. Challenge each class member to write a paragraph finishing the sentence, "I belong to the Church of the Brethren because . . . ." If time permits, share your answers with one another.

Chapter 2

1. Discuss the word "unity." What does it suggest to you? Does it mean the same as uniformity, i.e. sameness, or is there a deeper meaning?

2. Debate the proposition: "Resolved: We are all members of one universal family." You could have two presenters for each side, pro and con, and a moderator. The rest of the class could act as judges. Alternate pro and con arguments, giving each presenter two minutes for initial arguments, then one minute for a summary (or rebuttal).

The team in favor of the proposition may want to cite:
—our faith that one God has created us all.

—the biblical dream of one family under God.
—scientific and cultural evidence for one human family.
—successful inter-cultural and inter-racial marriages.
—the interdependence of all people on earth.
The team rejecting the proposition may want to:
—highlight cultural and physical differences.
—refer to the Tower of Babel story.
—note that blacks and whites alike tend to gather with their
    own kind.
—argue that God's attempt to make a general covenant with
    humankind did not work.
—appeal to the individual differences in taste and ability of
    class members.
Allow time for a period of debriefing following the debate.
Share your real convictions on the issue.

3. Discuss whether the world is closer to being a family now
than it was in the time of the prophets. Support your answer
with some specific illustrations.

4. Discuss: Are modern day nations, with their strong
patriotic ties, deterrents to the unity of humankind? How could
they be helpful agents of unity?

5. Describe a situation in which you made friends with or
associated with a person or persons from another nation and
culture. Was the person easy to accept as a "brother" or "sister"?
What were your feelings as you talked with the person?

Chapter 3

1. To experience some of the drama of the incident at Jacob's
well ask each class member to read silently John 4:1-20, then
write on a piece of paper his or her personal answers to the
following questions:
—How would you describe Jesus' physical condition as you
    feel it in verse 6?
—How do you picture the woman's clothing in your im-
    agination? Bright, gayly colored? Dull, ragged? Simple,
    neat?
—If you were the woman would you have complied with the
    stranger's request for water? Why or why not?
—What emotion did you identify as the woman's when Jesus
    alluded to her adultery?
—If you had been one of the disciples would you have want-

ed to know what Jesus and the woman were talking about?

—What do you think occurred in the woman's concept of herself that caused her to run to the city in verses 28-29.

Share your answers with each other in smaller groups of three or four persons each. Let each person state his or her response to the first question, then do the same for the second, etc.

2. Jesus disregarded racial, social, sexual, and national barriers in the examples cited in this session. Discuss this material. Were there other points of division which Jesus attacked and to which he spoke? How do Jesus' attitudes and actions relate to the ecumenical vision of a reunited human family?

3. Do you agree with the statement that "if Jesus were choosing the Twelve today there would in all likelihood be some women among the group?" Why do you think he did not choose some women then for the original band?

Chapter 4

1. Review the highlights of the story of the early church in Acts as it relates to the theme of this chapter:

—In what ways did the early Christians in Jerusalem experience unity?

—As the new family expanded, how did it show itself to be an *inclusive* family. What specific barriers were broken down?

—How does the early church begin to fulfill the promise of God to Abraham in Genesis 12:1-3? (See chapter 2, pp. 21-22.)

2. Note the new relationship of trust among the first century Christians, enabling them to move freely from group to group. Does your congregation welcome visitors with such acceptance? Can persons from other denominations who seek membership in your congregation break into the fellowship easily?

3. The church at Antioch was cosmopolitan in nature, probably embracing persons of different races as well as nationalities. Examine your own congregation's policies of membership admission. Is your fellowship open to *all* persons? Apart from policy is there genuine acceptance of all regardless of race and creed?

4. List the threshholds in your community that are the most difficult for you as self-respecting proud individuals to cross. Are

there slum houses, cocktail bars, political offices, miser mansions, etc. that contain persons outside the Christian family? Do you have a responsibility to witness to and serve them?

5. Review the words to the popular folk hymn, "They'll Know We Are Christians By Our Love," No. 6 in *The Brethren Songbook*. Do the verses describe the true intention of your church? Of yourself? Perhaps you would want to sing the hymn as a closing for this session.

Chapter 5

1. Review some of the "domestic squabbles and family splits" described in this session. Were divisions such as these inevitable? Why or why not?

2. Do a simulation of the so-called Council of Jerusalem, reenacting its deliberations on the question of whether circumcision could be waived in order for Gentiles to become Christians. You will need at the outset to divide into three groups:

> The delegation from Antioch
> The Christian Pharisees
> The other elders and apostles

Each group should read Acts 15:1-30, then determine its strategy in the Council. The following information may be helpful:

The delegation from Antioch is presenting the case for no circumcision. Paul and Barnabas are the principal spokesmen (elect someone to be each). You will want to argue that Christianity supersedes Judaism, but be tactful enough so as not to make matters worse. You may want to refer to the call to Abraham to be the father of *all* nations (Gen. 12), and the ingathering of new members to Israel (Isa. 44:4-5). Of course you will want to argue that Jesus put people before tradition. Perhaps you will want someone to do some behind-the-scenes negotiating with the "other elders and apostles" group, who are undecided in their vote.

The Christian Pharisees are those who want to retain as much of Jewish tradition as possible in Christianity and insist that the only way to Christianity is through Judaism. James, the bishop of Jerusalem and maybe the brother of Jesus, will be the chief spokesman. (Be sure you elect someone to be James.) James will also preside over the Council and will insist on a roll call vote. You, the Pharisees, will stress a strong allegiance to Judaism and insist upon discipline as the key to commitment. You may want someone to do some behind-the-scenes negotiating with the "other elders and apostles" group who are undecided in their vote.

The other elders and apostles will probably decide the issue. As a group you will not take a stand either way before the council meeting. But Peter is in your group (elect someone to be Peter), and his influence is strong. You have heard Peter's story about Cornelius and you anticipate hearing it again. In fact, you insist on Peter telling it in the council. Since, however, there may be some disagreement within your group, you may wish for the council to reach a consensus rather than taking a vote.

Allow ten minutes for the groups to prepare for the Council. Then James will convene the Council. *Note:* it is not necessary to come out exactly as did the first century Jerusalem Council! You may decide differently!

Be sure to take at least ten minutes following the simulation for a debriefing period. Share your feelings about the experience, including the roles you assumed.

3. Take a look at your congregation from the standpoint of social and doctrinal differences. Is there a tendency for groups to form and compete with other groups or the rest of the church? Is there a "Christ Party"—a group, whether organized or not, which thinks it is always right?

4. You may want to use in connection with this session the filmstrip on "The Council of Nicaea." (See Appendix 1 for a listing of audio-visual resources and where they can be obtained.)

Chapter 6

1. Consider Paul's contribution as a peacemaker and mediator in the churches he founded. In addition to the passages mentioned in the text, see Galatians 5:26-6:10, Ephesians 4:25-32, and 1 Corinthians 1:10-17, 26-30. In each instance, Paul is urging some gap-bridging within the churches for whom he feels responsible. Divide your class into three groups and assign each group one of the scriptures. Ask each group to identify and list the ways Paul suggests in the assigned text for working at unity. Let each group report to the total class. (Don't hesitate to try this if your class is small. The minimum requirement for a group is two!)

2. Heritage is obviously a valuable asset for maintaining unity in the church. What common Christian traditions (worship, ministerial, leadership, etc.) would you cite as threads which run consistently through each century of Christianity?

3. Review the author's documentation of the "gathering storm" between 1800 and 1920 that led to the modern ecumenical movement. List on the chalkboard or newsprint the factors that gave impetus to the ecumenical train. What factors of human existence today make ecumenical cooperation necessary?

4. Air the feelings of the class as to whether all Protestants should be in one all-encompassing church. Would it work? Where do you foresee difficulties? Strengths?

5. What changes in the past ten years have you noticed in the relationships between Protestants and Roman Catholics? What percentage of your class has been inside of a Catholic church? Attended a Mass? Would your discovery merit the planning of a field trip to a Roman Catholic service, or perhaps the services of other communions you are not familiar with?

6. The audio-visual resources listed in Appendix 1 include several filmstrips featuring the work of the World and National Councils. You may want to use one or more with this session.

Chapter 7

1. The first part of this session's material suggests that the space age has revolutionized human life for the seventies. Has the church felt these changes as challenges to its witness and belief? To its survival? How has the church responded? Discuss the current emphasis in ecumenical activity outlined in this chapter as they relate to this changed situation.

2. Is your congregation already working at conciliar relations with other churches as defined in this session—mutual regard for members and ministers, full communion (meaning that your church and other churches are meeting sacramentally at some point), mutual help, joint programs and actions? Make a list of specific instances.

3. Organize within your class a debate on the topic: "Resolved: Denominationalism Is Not a Deterent to Church Unity." Select two persons each for the positive and negative sides. Have each person make two one-minute arguments, alternating sides. Let the rest of the class serve as judges to determine which side presents the most convincing case.

Points for the positive side might be:
- —Polity and rites do not need to be uniform.
- —There is much that denominations can agree on and do together.
- —A united voice is imperative in today's world and can be achieved without giving up individual traditions.
- —Each communion's uniqueness can contribute toward a better whole.

Points for the negative side might be:
- —Each denomination wants to do things its way.
- —There can be no unity until all Christians can sit together for the same meal at the Lord's table.
- —There is too much diversity among denominations to achieve any substantive agreement on anything.
- —The only way to assure true unity is through merger.

4. Is your congregation in relationship to *all* other bodies of faith in your area, or are you selective in your choice of non-Brethren brothers and sisters? Is there a church nearby with whom you should establish contact? Could your class initiate it in some way?

5. Is there something undesirable in your community that could perhaps be remedied if all the congregations in the area joined in witness (a tavern, pornographic movies, neglected juveniles, deteriorating housing, etc.)? Discuss how, as a class, you might initiate a cooperative effort to correct the situation.

Chapter 8

1. Discuss the advantages and disadvantages you see in Brethren retaining a distinct identity. Why did Brethren of an earlier day feel the need to stand apart from others? How does this relate to our situation today? Do you view Annual Conference as a "defensive" gathering, or as an event which enhances the denomination's sense of belonging to the larger church family?

2. List the Brethren that you know personally who are involved in the leadership of a cooperative, interfaith organization. Don't forget even the local cluster or church-sponsored community agency. Interview one or two of these persons as to why and how they became involved in an ecumenical venture. Ask them their opinion of the future of the Church of the Brethren in ecumenism.

3. Read the entire statement made by J. W. Lear to the council of Boards of the Church of the Brethren in 1928. (See Appendix 2 for the full text.) Do his statements have relevance for today?

4. The "associated relationship" between the Brethren and the American Baptists has worked well for both groups. Do you think the denomination ought to enter into a similar relationship with other communions? Support your answer.

5. Examine the models cited in which Brethren have been involved in congregations united across denominational lines, then discuss these comments by participants in these congregations:

"There was a time when I wondered if Christianity could transcend its differences . . . "

"Union has forced us all to rethink what tradition and church membership means and helped us appreciate it more."

"It is difficult to interpret to the children how they can be Mennonite and Brethren at the same time."

6. Ask your pastor if there is a past or present member of the Committee on Interchurch Relations who lives in or close to your area. If so, you might invite that person to come to your class and share further the committee's current activity. Don't hesitate to ask. The members will welcome the opportunity, no matter what size class you have!

7. Discuss whether there are any persons in your class or congregation who may be good nominees for the Committee on Interchurch Relations. Give your suggestions to your pastor, who will forward them to the proper Annual Conference nominating committee.

Chapter 9

1. Place the statements of Warren Groff and Floyd Mitchell on pp. 81 and 87 on newsprint or a chalkboard. Do you agree that just being Brethren commits us to work for the unity of the church? As you discuss this question, list and reflect on the features of the "Brethren consciousness" mentioned in this session.

2. Examine the story of the prodigal son (Luke 15:11-32). Draw an analogy between the story and the issue of church unity. What attitudes toward church cooperation and interfaith fellowship would each of the three principals (father, younger son, elder son) represent? Which attitude do you think best

typifies the Brethren?

3. Divide the class into four groups and assign to each group one of the problem situations below. Give them ten minutes to work at how they would handle the situations, then assemble again as a class to hear and discuss the report of each group. Do your responses illustrate the Brethren consciousness spoken of earlier?

Situation 1: You are the hospitality committee of your church. It has been pointed out that the Grabowski family, the newest members of the church, are feeling a bit strange among the Millers, Bowmans, and Garbers. The pastor has asked you to do what you can to make them feel at home.

Situation 2: Three members of the church board, all of whom joined the congregation from other denominations, request the institution of bread and cup communions on Sunday mornings, in addition to the full love feast which is held twice a year. They express a sincere desire to renew this form of sacrament which was meaningful in their past. Others on the Board express fear this may reduce attendance at love feast. How would you resolve the issue?

Situation 3: You are the executive committee faced with a major decision. The date for the annual Share the Faith Ecumenical Service of the local cluster of churches falls on the traditional date for your congregation's most successful fellowship program of the year. You have already started publicity and work on the program. However, all of the other congregations have cleared the date for the interfaith service. What will you do?

Situation 4: Your Commission on Witness has learned that a recent wind storm extensively damaged the roof of the neighboring Roman Catholic Church, and that they need volunteer help to be able to make the necessary repairs. You are aware of some very strong feeling within your congregation that Catholic parochial school aid is seriously limiting adequate funds for the local public school program. Some feel "we've already done enough for them." What should you do?

4. Should Brethren use the terms "Brother" and "Sister" in addressing non-Brethren Christians? Non-Christians? Why or why not? Does the doctrine of universal restoration held by earlier Brethren apply here?

5. Examine the words of the hymn, "Christ for the World We

Sing" (No. 559 in *The Brethren Hymnal*). Do they express your class's concept of mission?

Chapter 10

1. Study Colossians 3:12-17 and 1 Peter 3:8-17, which were mentioned in the text as primary resources on congregational unity. List as a class the virtues that make for unity according to each passage. Discuss the importance of thanksgiving for a sense of unity.

2. Review the material on 1 Corinthians, noting the threats to unity which the Corinthians experienced and the way Paul speaks to the situation in chapters 12 and 13. Building on the image of the church as a body, invite class members to list for themselves and others in the class the part of the human body that best expresses the gifts they bring to the life of the church. (An eye, for example, could represent helping others to see things more clearly, or being on the lookout for those overlooked, etc.) Share your lists with one another.

3. Discuss the author's statement that the average congregation tends to measure the value of persons (members) by their function. Is this true in your congregation? Or do you honor an usher as much as the moderator?

4. Discuss the love feast as an illustration of the unity we seek. What effect does the love feast have for your church? Can it be a unifying experience even though less than half of the "family" attends? Did the deacon visit before love feast serve the purpose of encouraging unity? Did it work? Would you encourage its practice again?

5. Are there particular tensions or conflicts which threaten or block unity in your congregation? If so, identify them, reflect on their origin, and project ways of dealing with them constructively.

Chapter 11

1. React to the position that there is a place within the church for groups that champion a certain cause. Do you agree or disagree? What criteria does this chapter set up for helping such groups maintain a constructive relationship to the total church fellowship? Would you add other qualifications?

2. Reflect on our Brethren heritage in dealing with dissent. Should we return to the practice of requiring full consensus on a decision before we accept it? What are the reasons for member

apathy when it comes to attendance at congregational business meetings? Do you heartily agree that "for Brethren people are more important than ideologies?" Any examples to support your answer?

3. Note the various subgroups in our Brethren family at the present time. At what points do each of these groups have something to give to the whole church? If members of the class actively relate to one or more of these groups, practice the way of dialogue by encouraging them to share their concerns. An example of such a concern would be the Womaen's Caucus' call for equal apportionment of women and men in the leadership positions at all levels of the church; a change in language that consistently uses masculine words to denote God and other persons; and redefinition of the roles for men and women, wives and husbands, that does not stereotype either in authority or function. Are you responsive to such concerns in your congregation?

4. If possible, secure copies of volume 21 of *Brethren Life and Thought*. Examine together the list of divisions listed by Blair and Long (specifically the Winter 1976 issue, pp. 29-32). Pay particular attention to the precipitating causes. How can the church today prevent further divisions from occuring in its life and fellowship?

5. Below is an item called "A Feminist's Ten Commandments," copyrighted by the Omaha chapter of the National Organization of Women, 1975. Discuss in your class the relevance they have for writing ten commandments for an ecumenist:

1. Thou shalt not let disagreement become dissension and thou shalt learn to distinguish between the two.

2. Thou shalt have a singlemindedness of purpose in working for the betterment of women's status, keeping in mind that self-interest is the greatest motivator.

3. Thou shalt not recognize failure, neither shalt thou accept partial success.

4. Thou shalt support thy sister and understand that humanness necessitates error.

5. Thou shalt not let power become thy goal, but rather the benefits that power brings.

6. Thou shalt not force thy expectations on another person, nor allow another to force you into their expectations.

7. Thou shalt accept ALL PERSONS as individuals with rights equal to those you would have recognized for you.

8. Thou shalt not fear to be forceful when force is called for, neither

shalt thou fear to be gentle when gentleness is called for.

9. Thou shalt remember that one woman cannot change the world, but many working together with purposeful direction can accomplish miracles.

10. Above all, thou shalt recognize that if you get it all together, it may all come apart!

Chapter 12

1. Discuss how the accountability we share in our genetic families applies to the accountability which should exist between denominations. How do your family members "answer to or report to" other members of the family in a responsible, caring, sharing way?

2. Discuss: By what means do the various communions in your area communicate and fellowship? Is there a council of churches or similar organization. Do you know what it does? What could happen in your community if the churches of your area combined their resources and leadership for action? Can you list some things? Does anything on your list seem like an idea you could pursue now?

3. Section II of the report of the Nairobi Assembly of the World Council of Churches, entitled "What Unity Requires," recommends that "all churches should encourage and assist their members in regular and informed intercession for the other churches." They should further provide for "reciprocal visitation among the churches for the purpose of sharing in each other's liturgy, theology, and spirituality, and for mutual help, counsel, and encouragement." As initial steps in this direction, you might:

—Use the litany found in the appendices, Appendix 3.

—Appoint a committee to discuss with the pastor and worship committee the possibility of a pulpit and choir exchange with a neighboring church, with the visiting pastor planning the worship. Or simply exchange delegations to each other's church service.

4. Try the following simulation. Divide the class into four groups, representing Lutherans, Presbyterians, Brethren, and Pentecostal Holiness. Your task as a total group is to plan a cooperative Thanksgiving service of worship.

Each denominational group will come to the planning meeting with some preconceived ideas about what kind of service would be appropriate. Each group should caucus prior to the

141

planning session to work out its strategy. The following information may be helpful:

—The Lutherans are used to a prescribed ritual and a formal service. The hymns are majestic. There is much congregational response.

—the Presbyterians are conscious of the importance of religion in the development of the national character. They believe in strong preaching as the central focus in worship. The Apostles Creed is always used in their Sunday morning worship services. They are used to having their own services on Thanksgiving morning.

—The Brethren do not understand the creeds and do not care for such. They frequently use the Lord's Prayer, however. They would like to stress the importance of continual work for peace and feel Thanksgiving would be a good time to promote brotherhood with all people. They would rather sing some of the hymns from the "Songs of Salvation" section of the Brethren hymnal, but as long as peace is mentioned in the service they will not insist on their hymns. There are quite a few Brethren family gatherings on Thanksgiving Day.

—The Pentecostal Holiness have a rather free-wheeling service of worship. They do not use bulletins and they read from the *Living Bible*. They believe in the direction of the Holy Spirit and the opportunity to give everyone in the congregation a chance to share concerns—a prayer, a testimony, etc. They support the local city mission and take services to the mission twice a week.

Give each group ample time to discuss its strategy, then come together for the meeting. After electing a chairperson, proceed to take up the agenda for the meeting. You will want to come to agreement as to:

—Where the service will be held.
—When (Thanksgiving eve, the Sunday before, Thanksgiving Day???)
—What kind of service.
—What order of service.
—Who will preach (if there is preaching).
—Special music (choir—guest choir, combined choir, one of the churches provide a choir???)
—Will there be an offering and how shall it be distributed?

(*Note*: This simulation could take an entire period. You may want to plan it as next week's class. If so, group members could be chosen in advance and could discover more information about their respective "denominations" for input into their role play.)

Chapter 13

1. On the following page is a continuum showing how values change as the religious consciousness of a group moves from sectarianism to global community, as this study hopes its readers will do. The movement is from left to right on the continuum. Each structural form is evaluated for its spirit, relationships to other religious communities, and degree of trust.

Where would you place your congregation on the continuum? The Church of the Brethren? Where would you *like* to be?

2. Do you agree that the Christian church is the primary catalyst for the unity of humankind? Does the promise of God to bring about a family reunion of the nations through Abraham and his descendents apply? How do the texts discussed in this chapter help us answer the question?

3. Discuss Archimandrite Argenti's statement, "If we are not united, we are not the church." Do you see unity within the church as a prerequisite before the church can be about the agenda of world needs? Should we "set our own house in order" first, or will that be too late?

4. Do you believe the list of global concerns suggested by the Nairobi Assembly is complete? Would you add or subtract any items?

5. To what extent does your congregation exhibit a consciousness of the global community and work to improve it. List ways by which your congregation can work at global concerns right within your community. What organizations for change and human rights can you work with, contributing support and personnel from the church? What international humanitarian agencies does your church or individuals within your church support?

6. Use the filmstrip, "The Hungry Future," to dramatize the imperative of global concern. (See Appendix 1 for information on ordering this and other filmstrips.)

	Inflexibility		Flexibility		
Structure:	Sect	Denominations	Interdenominational Cooperation	Ecumenicity	Global Community
Spirit:	Developing a distinct and self-oriented identity	Consolidating and maintaining an autonomous identity	Working together in spite of separate identities	Contributing to or drawing from each other's identities	Affirming common identity in the midst of diversity
Relation to Others:	Separateness	Defensiveness Competitiveness	Openness	Accountability	Mutuality
Trust level with respect to others:	Radical Distrust	Skepticism	Guarded Trust	Vulnerability	Total Trust